Praise for
Simple Ways ...

"This book is a practi... ... the mother of four, I know the pressures ... ...sica Teich and Brandel France de Bravo help relocate the values of listening, seeing, and sharing the discovery of each day with a child."

—Meryl Streep

"The authors speak with a warmth and clarity that reassures and informs parents just when they need it most. Theirs is a deft, appreciated touch in the shouting match that so often characterizes parenting books."

—Kyle D. Pruett, M.D., Clinical Professor of Child Psychiatry, Yale University, and author of *Me, Myself and I: How Children Build Their Sense of Self*

"A light and lovely Zen-influenced collection. . . . Their practical advice is peppered with loving reminders that for may mothers, life is too pressured and too fast."

—*Fit Pregnancy*

"In our fast-paced, high-pressure world, it's easy to get drawn into a stressful, painstaking form of parenting. In this lovely little book, Jessica Teich and Brandel France de Bravo remind us that the best parenting is often simple and instinctive—and they give practical ideas for helping parents stay present and see the wonder and connection, even when changing diapers."

—Richard Carlson, Ph.D., author of *Don't Sweat the Small Stuff*

trees

make the best mobiles

simple ways to raise your child in a complex world

jessica teich

and

brandel france de bravo

St. Martin's Griffin
New York

www.stmartins.com

Library of Congress Cataloging-in-Publication Data

Teich, Jessica.
    Trees make the best mobiles: simple ways to raise your child in a complex world / Jessica Teich and Brandel France de Bravo.
        p. cm.
    ISBN 0-312-26930-7 (hc)
    ISBN 0-312-30325-4 (pbk)
    1. Infants—Care. 2. Toddlers—Care. 3. Parenting. 4. Parent and infant. I. France de Bravo, Brandel. I. Title.

HO774 .T43 2001
649'.122—dc21   2001041813

10 9 8 7 6 5 4 3

for isabel and amaya,

our daughters and teachers,

and

for their fathers,

michael and mario

contents

acknowledgments

❦

Writing a book is a bit like birthing a baby. It's a lot harder than you think, and the result never looks quite like you'd imagined. Our labor had the benefit of many midwives, first and foremost our agent Brian DeFiore, who believed in the project even when it had a very different title and tone, and who answered our every question with patience and clarity. Other early supporters include our editor, Elizabeth Beier, who hung in there with us even as we moved cities, changed schools, left the country for long periods, and extended an early deadline. We also owe thanks to our mothers, Suzanne Teich and Ruth France, who read the manuscript in an early incarnation and did not disown it, or us.

We are greatly indebted to two other readers: Daniel Wolfe, who gave us the benefit of his long experience as a writer, and offered specific and valuable comments on our first finished draft, and Michael Gendler, who graciously accepted the role of "critic-in-residence," and served as our lawyer during the search for a book agent. Our thanks and love also to Aida L. Jaco, who kept our daughters company while we worked, fed them (and us), and nurtured them even as we would have had we been there. We are grateful to our mentors: the visionary founder of RIE, Magda Gerber; our RIE instructors, Elizabeth Memel and Carol Pinto; Mary Hartzell Rota for her practical advice; Gurmukh for her teachings, both spiritual and mundane; Hasmik Avetisian and Julie Kern for their love of reading and the arts, and Judy Accardi and all the teachers at Play Mountain Place for emphasizing the importance of feelings, especially to the very young. These women are godmothers to our book, and we hope we did them proud. Finally, our thanks to all the friends who called to see how we (and the book) were doing: Toby Appleton, Janet S. Blake, Jennifer Clement, Victoria Godfrey, Bonni Goldberg, Gabriel Ramirez, Elizabeth Sherwood-Randall, and Rosanne State. It takes a village to write a book as well.

p r e f a c e

People in movies tend to "meet cute," when their dog leashes become entangled or they swap suitcases by accident. New parents have their own version of this time-honored ritual. It's called "meeting low." They are digging with their children in the sandbox, or putting on shoes at preschool, or sitting cross-legged on the floor at story time. We, too, met on the floor, of a yoga center in Los Angeles, where we were attending an unusual parenting course. In the movies the couple falls in love, has some madcap adventures, argues, and resolves their differences by the closing, soon-to-be-Oscar-nominated song. We fell in "like," compared notes on our careers as writers, and began talking about writing the kind of parenting book we longed for but could never find.

We discovered, during that first talk, that we and our friends needed parenting books that respected us as sentient beings, tired though we were. We're *all* mothers who think and care and wonder and worry. What we're not is people with lots of time on our hands. We began to imagine a book that would tackle some of the toughest challenges of parenting, without becoming one of those "exhaustive" books on child-rearing that become exhausting to read. We believe that all parents want to thrive in concert with their children and that, although nine months can seem an eternity when your feet swell or your stomach revolts, it's never enough time to become the parent you want to be.

The result is an intuitive and eclectic approach to raising children, based largely on observation and experience. Our book advises you to do less, listen more, speak directly to your newborn, involve your infant in her own care, and treat this mewling creature with the same respect you treat your partner, and yourself. These principles may seem simple, even self-evident, yet often the simplest tasks invite our mind to wander or our patience to flag. Our child may beckon to us, and although we respond, what we're really thinking is, "What's in the refrigerator for dinner?" or "When can I return that call?" We call our approach "present parenting," because the idea of being *present in the moment* is its guiding light. As parents, we tend to focus on what's ahead, what we need to accomplish, even resorting to bribes or threats to expedite our goal. What children really want is someone to be with them *now*—not to judge, or even to participate, but to observe. They want to know we're there: respectful, relaxed, engaged but not overbearing. For them, our presence, our focus, is our greatest gift.

Our book addresses the years from birth to preschool, but many of its insights apply to early adolescence as well. It is intended for all parents—whether they have twenty minutes to spend with their baby at the end of a long workday or are on duty 24/7. Present parenting isn't an esoteric set of ideals, but a highly practical program for investing the most routine tasks, like feeding and bathing, with humor and tenderness. It will help make time with your child richer and more rewarding. We believe even changing a diaper can change your life.

Yet most new parents—the two of us included—have little time to reflect on their actions. They barely have time to mail a letter or wash a sock. Our hope is that parents will take our advice to heart when they can, as often as they can. Even used briefly, and sporadically, present parenting can have benefits. Every time you respect your child's initiative—allowing her to reach for a toy on her own, or figure out how something works—you bolster her sense of competence. Every time you sit on the floor with her, even for ten minutes a day, and discover how *she* wishes to play, or just watch silently, you learn more about her than any baby book can ever teach.

As parents, we are frequently humbled by the daily demands of caring for a child. That, and our curiosity, led us to the class in which we met. The program, based on the teachings of Magda Gerber, is called Resources for Infant Educarers, or RIE. It was founded in Los Angeles in 1978. Now in her eighties, Ms. Gerber has reimagined infant and toddler care much as Maria Montessori did education for nursery-age children. Ms. Gerber was among the first child-development specialists to suggest that even very young babies should participate in their own care and that parents who interfere unduly, when safety is not an issue, can make their children dependent and insecure. After attending RIE classes for the duration of the two-year program, we supplemented our training with courses in communication skills and conflict resolution, and workshops taught by international experts like Adele Faber and Amelia Gambetti.

These classes helped us consider questions of independence and respect that interested us as parents, family members, and friends. Neither of us has a degree in child development. We were able to look at parenting through fresh eyes. In fact, we wanted to help other parents *see* differently by considering their choices and reactions from their child's point of view. We believe that child rearing begins at birth, and that even the tiniest infant is competent and resourceful. Every time you interact with your baby, you get a chance to teach him, to learn about him, and to encourage his autonomy and sense of accomplishment.

Our approach can liberate parents from feeling as though they must do *for* their babies, or *to* them, all the time. When we first met, our daughters, who are three months apart in age, were still lying on their backs on a big mat on the floor. Surrounding them were the simplest toys—plastic colanders and hair curlers from the five-and-ten—they could pick up and investigate if they wished. Or they could simply lie there, looking up. Our strong recommendation to new parents that they buy less, and invest in toys that *do* less, was informed by the delight our daughters took simply in *being*. To this day, they are happier reading, singing, or making things with paper and scissors than they would be playing with toys so sophisticated they make the human genome project look like child's play. It was from them that we learned to examine every pebble, to treat every shadow on the wall as a storyboard. They taught us that a tree outside the window can become a mobile, if we forgo the cheery, disposable *stuff* that litters the landscape of childhood in contemporary life.

Yet our own childhoods were populated by Twinkies and troll dolls, and the drone of the television formed a perpetual soundtrack. In many ways, our upbringing was typical of our generation and our background, at least in terms of education, was fairly traditional. Jessica graduated from Yale and Oxford, where she was a Rhodes scholar, and later received a filmmaking grant from the American Film Institute. For ten years, she worked in regional theatres as a dramaturg, developing and producing plays. Jessica's work in the theatre was strangely kindred to the process of parenting: Sitting in a rehearsal room for hours on end, as a playwright struggled to find his voice (or just make his jokes funnier), was unusually apt preparation for the practice of letting your toddler articulate her own point of view. The less visible the hand of the dramaturg, the more successful her participation. That, too, has something in common with parenting.

In addition to being a published poet, Brandel has a Master's in Public Health from Columbia University. She has worked in AIDS education and family planning all over the world and, in recent years, has expanded her health career to include labor support for pregnant women. Oddly enough, it was weathering a two-year-old's tantrums that best prepared Brandel for her work as a birth *doula*: While few of us would tell a laboring woman, "Stop crying and get over it!," some people think nothing of minimizing a child's physical and emotional pain.

Our experiences and intuitions are presented here with the support of extensive research, on everything from computer use in the schools to the optimal age at which to buy a plastic potty for your child. Each chapter is brief enough for you to dip into while your baby naps or before you put *yourself* down to sleep. But the chapters are meaty enough to get you thinking, and thinking differently, about your choices. We have addressed a range of issues, from sleeping and sharing to caregivers and coparenting, that plague new parents and add to the tensions in their home. Your baby will, eventually, stop teething, but most other concerns, especially when they involve discipline and self-control, recur throughout childhood. You may find insight into your four-month-old from a chapter about siblings, or become reacquainted with your five-year-old's need for autonomy when your read about thumb-sucking or toilet use. Don't feel you need to read the book straight through, chapter by chapter; rather, sample the chapters that satisfy your current hunger, or that provide a taste of the challenges that lie ahead.

Just as we urge parents not to dwell on the future, we encourage them not to focus on the past. We believe no parenting "mistake" is so great it can't be recovered from, and no strategy so indelible it can't be revised. Our children are surprisingly flexible and resilient. They *want* to live harmoniously with us. They offer us a chance, not only to quell past demons, but to leave behind the pressures of the day. With them, we can be our best selves: alert, vibrant, and generous—and fully alive in the present tense.

the anatomy lesson

 There's a Zen Buddhist saying, "Haste is a form of violence." As parents, we rarely leave ourselves enough time. Our children sense our frenzy and are unnerved by it. Often they become upset and *less* cooperative, which leads to more rushing. Think of every activity as a chance to slow down, to fill the moment with your concentration and care. Even changing a diaper can become—dare we say it?—pleasurable. It's a moment to connect with your child, especially if you've been away from each other all day. Don't use toys or a mobile to distract your newborn. Your eye contact is more compelling than any rattle. Think of diapering as an activity you engage in together, and tell him so: "Now we're going to change your diaper." Talk your infant through it, letting him know exactly what you are doing. Soon he may lift his legs ever so slightly in anticipation of a diaper change.

Changing your baby's diaper can be the equivalent of an anatomy lesson. He learns the contours of his body, that you and he are separate, and that his body belongs to him. The short-term goal of a diaper change is, of course, obvious, especially if your baby has been eating asparagus. But the long-term objective is profound: to involve your baby in the most intimate details of his nurture and care.

Let even the smallest infant feel he is in charge. Later, when he's older, you'll need his collaboration: A mobile child can easily scurry away. Toilet training, or learning, follows inevitably from your child's sense of participation. When he's of appropriate age—and most children under age two haven't developed the sphincter muscles for wearing underwear—start to talk to him about using the potty, and invite him to tell you when he's dirty or wet. Involve him in the changing of diapers, and let him fetch the new diaper or wipes. You may even consult him about location: "Would you like to be changed on the changing table or the floor?" Or perhaps he's just mastered walking and cherishes his verticality. Acknowledge his independence by asking, "Would you like to change your diaper lying down or standing up?"

No child attends his high school prom in a rented burgundy tuxedo and Pampers. When he's ready, when he can predict and control his body's movements, he'll leave his diapers behind. Meanwhile, make the task as pleasant, and as mutual, as you can. Don't rush through it. Changing a diaper isn't a chore; it's an opportunity.

i want
to be alone

the need for solitude

In the first three months of life, your baby will be as mysterious as Greta Garbo. "Is he passing gas or smiling at me?" This transition period—in which adults tread the choppy waters of parenthood, and the one-time fetus adjusts to leaving the womb—has been referred to as the fourth trimester. During this period parents, and especially mothers, feel they must hold their babies all the time.

Holding your newborn is one of life's greatest joys and privileges. Do it when you can devote yourself to it fully and savor the closeness. With the possible exception of a colicky infant, most babies do not need to be held all the time. Many new parents carry their infant from room to room and even take showers with the baby in a car seat on the bath

4

mat. Car seats are necessary and lifesaving . . . in the car. There's very little risk of whiplash in your bathroom.

As parents of newborns, we assume our babies are fragile, incompetent, and utterly dependent. We think they cannot survive without us. But they can. In 1985, Mexico City suffered one of the worst earthquakes in its history. Thousands died and whole buildings collapsed like accordions, including the maternity wards of two public hospitals. More than a week passed before rescue workers arrived to sift through the rubble. Imagine their surprise, and joy, when they discovered fifty-six newborns, bruised and hungry, but alive. These babies had survived unimaginable trauma. They did so on their own, with no baby monitor in sight.

If your baby is flat on his back on the floor in a safe area, or in a playpen or crib, it's okay to leave him alone for a few minutes. After all, the umbilical cord was severed for a reason. In fact, he may prefer being left alone to constantly being moved about and introduced to new surroundings. Besides, wouldn't you like a little time alone yourself? If your baby gets some private time he'll learn to need it. A child who cherishes solitude is likely to become an adult who's rarely lonely.

Every year the citizens of Mexico celebrate the birthday of the "earthquake babies" as if it were a national holiday. Believe in the daily miracle of life. Life—especially in the form of your infant—will not disappoint.

the long
and the short

Our children are our darlings. We adore them. We dote on them. Every juice spill is a Jackson Pollock. Every trill is an aria. But we all have days when we can't wait to hand off the baby like a ticking bomb, when we stare at the door, willing another grown-up to appear.

Child rearing is the world's second oldest profession, but it's a job for which few of us feel qualified. What's more, few of us have the time to be the parents we want to be: Every art project gets shelved when the toilet overflows. But sometimes it's straddling the two realms—yours and your child's—that's most exhausting. Plunging headlong into your child's world can be a relief. Try to immerse yourself fully in what your child's doing, even

7

for twenty minutes, even just once a day. That single focus is what your child craves. Let her know she's not competing for your attention with the grocery list or with your assignment for tomorrow's meeting with a client. Just sit against the wall and watch her gurgle or play, or get down to her level on the floor. Don't feel you need to interact, especially to direct or stimulate her. Imagine how you would feel if your spouse barged in on you, grabbed the novel you were reading, and insisted you take tango lessons instead?

There's a saying, "If you want to get something done, ask a busy person to do it." That's true . . . except if you're a child. Getting things done isn't the goal of very young children. Very young children simply want to *be*. It's difficult for highly accomplished and efficient people to put down their palm pilot, just as it's difficult to shutter one's ambitions for one's child. But children don't want to have to perform for you, especially when they're playing. They simply want to know a grown-up is there. They may not acknowledge your presence, but they'll take pleasure in it. This is the *real* quality time: time simply to be. In truth, you, too, may welcome a chance to throw off the pressures of the day. With your child, you don't have to be organized, capable, *adult*.

Soon it'll be your child who has places to go (if only to the mall). Every charming, beckoning toddler becomes a teenager. Each time you say, "I just need another minute to finish this . . . ," you squander a moment with your child, never to be reclaimed. Remember, the days are long, but the years are very short.

baby talk

Yyy-eee-sss, you ARE! You ARE the cutest! I'm gonna eat those toes-ies. Yyy-eee-sss, I will! Ohhh, whadisit? Mommy's little baby sleepy? Go night-night?

Stretching syllables, speaking in a high-pitched voice, and mimicking your baby's sounds can be fun, especially when it elicits a smile from your little one, but it's not everyone's cup of tea. If *goo-goo*, *ga-ga* is as foreign to you as a radio broadcast from Ougadougou, try this definition of "baby talk": It's talk directed to your baby, concerning her care. Whether you're feeding, bathing, diapering, or dressing your baby, give her a blow-by-blow account of what you're doing and let her know what she can do to help. Your newborn won't be able to give you a hand with the snaps on her "onesie," but it won't be long before she's

10

choosing—by pointing and grunting—between the tie-dye and the stripes.

What your baby *doesn't* need to hear about are the receipts you need for filing taxes or the items you're packing for a trip. If you're constantly thinking aloud, your baby may tune you out. You don't want to become the human equivalent of Lite FM.

Avoid talking about your baby as if she weren't there. If you need to brag or vent frustration, try addressing your comments to the friend or relative *and* your baby. Instead of saying, "Emily isn't a good sleeper," try "Neither of us is sleeping very well these days. Emily is waking every couple of hours. Isn't that right, Em?"

For someone new to the world, life is a bumpy ride, unpredictable and even treacherous. Your job is to pave the way. Think of your own visits to a doctor's office: One nurse jabs you with a needle, and the pain lasts minutes. Another explains that the alcohol swab is cool, that you'll feel a little prick, and that she's removing the needle now. Funny how the latter experience is painless or nearly so. That's because the "nice" nurse is talking you through the experience, helping you anticipate what's about to happen and make sense of what's just occurred. Too often we point out the poodle across the street, or exclaim at the ambulance shrieking past, never thinking to tell our little one about more mundane matters, like when we're simply going to lift her out of the stroller or strap her in.

Our babies, of course, do a much better job of this. Their cries prompt us to pick them up, but what cue do *we* give when we want to put our infant down or pass her to someone else to hold? Your baby needs a voice-over narration to explain what's happening *right now*, but she also deserves a preview of coming attractions: "In a minute, I'm going to give you to your grandmother. I have to go to the kitchen and fix dinner." Imagine leaving a movie theater, holding your husband's hand, when suddenly he yanks it away and you feel someone else's fingers—without a wedding band—fumbling to entwine themselves with yours. That's how your baby feels when you place her in another's arms without warning.

If your husband left the house nights without telling you, would you continue to trust him? For your baby to trust you, you must build that trust brick by brick. Telling the truth, even when it makes a child cry ("I'm going out now, but I'll be back in three hours"), is the mortar that holds the bricks together. Soon enough you'll need and expect the truth from your child: "A man at the park told me not to tell you, but . . ."

When the big, bad wolf of adolescence is at your door, you'll be glad you built a strong house.

safe at home

No creature comes with more stuff than your baby. Even before his or her arrival, you may feel overwhelmed by the number of things you "need." There are antiquated terms—what the heck is a layette?—and complex equipment whose instructions would tie a string-theory physicist in knots. New parents often feel that a squalling newborn should come with his own apartment, one with plenty of storage and soundproof tiles on all the walls. Certainly, as a new parent, your world expands, and you can feel your family line stretching forward into the new millennium. The only problem is, where are you gonna put all that stuff?

Don't forget that most infants can sleep contently in a sock drawer. They don't need a nursery stocked with the latest NASA-approved toys. What they do need is a safe play space, free of electrical cords, top-heavy televisions, and impulsive pets. You may love your glass-topped coffee table, but think about lending it to your sister for a year or two. Even parents whose homes shrink when baby takes up residence can close off a corner, securing it with a simple wooden barrier or gate. Think of the area as an oversized playpen, one your child won't easily outgrow. It's a place your infant should be introduced to before he's seen the world-at-large, meaning *before* he's had the run of the living room. Otherwise, he won't be content in it for long. He should regard the area as a haven, a meditation retreat, a study. It's not meant to be a prison cell.

You can begin this process about the time your baby is six months old, but don't put him in this space when he's tired or hungry. Before you leave him there for extended periods, spend some uninterrupted time there with him yourself. You may find this process works best if you attempt it at the same time every day, after breakfast, for example, or after a nap. As long as the space is safe, your infant can spend time alone there every day, free to lie on his back and think his thoughts. Soon, you may find yourself welcoming these interludes: You can use the time to answer phone calls or prepare a meal. When you're juggling your baby and other tasks, you're forever policing him, taking dangerous objects from his hands and mouth. If he's in a safe space, he's free from constant scrutiny, and you no longer have to monitor every move. A safe space means never having to say, "I'm sorry . . . you can't play with that." What's more, your baby will discover he's very good company to himself.

By devoting a safe space wholly to your infant, you will be freed from having to baby proof your entire home. It's still a good idea to put plastic covers on electrical outlets and to do so long before your child notices them. Always anticipate your child's explorations: Put a gate on the stairwell before he decides to scale Mount Everest. But children shouldn't be raised in a plastic bubble; their development and immune systems are bolstered by contact with their environment. What's more, you won't always be around to deter them from unsafe choices. Your job is to demonstrate how to interact with the world. Think of yourself as a tutor, not part of a SWAT team. Show him how to touch a glass gently or, with an older child, how to use scissors with care. If you must take something away from your child because it's unsafe, always do so with an explanation. That will help him make connections and may prevent him from picking up something inappropriate the next time. Be calm, clear, and complete: "That's a sharp knife. It can cut you, so I don't want you to play with it," or "Those pushpins are for the bulletin board. It looks like you want to put them in your mouth, but that's not safe."

Keep in mind that, for toddlers, safety means more than locking a door or securing a bottle top; it means giving them a safe space to explore their feelings, not just what's at their fingertips. Small children rely on their parents to help define the contours of their world, emotionally as well as physically. After a long day at preschool or in day care, a young child needs the chance to unwind, just as you do when you come home from work.

Adults may kick off their shoes or loosen their tie to ease the tensions of the day. Children, too, need a chance to let it all hang out. Being with a caregiver, or at school, requires enormous concentration for a small child. He really has to work at it; it's the equivalent of a job. Your child is greatly relieved to return to you at the end of the day because he doesn't have to be "on," to perform. Child psychologists say that the young patients they treat are rarely kids who have the freedom to "act out" at home.

That doesn't mean giving your child a license to mistreat you. His emotional breathing room, like any safe space, has very clear rules. Still, your child may push buttons with you that he wouldn't with anyone else. Before you blow your top, remember: It's a tribute to his trust in you. Robert Frost said, "Home is the place where, when you have to go there, they have to take you in." For small children, *you* are that home, that haven of acceptance and predictability. That your children "misbehave" with you, trust you with who they are when they are most monstrous, is the surest sign that they feel safe.

thumbs up

P. T. Barnum once said, "There's a sucker born every minute." But thanks to ultrasound, we now know we're suckers even *before* we're born. A fetus as young as eighteen weeks can be glimpsed with her thumb in her mouth. Once the umbilical cord is cut, babies suck to survive, as well as to calm themselves. It's safe to say that sustenance delivered by a nipple—human or artificial—is the original "comfort food."

The decision to breast- or bottle-feed your baby is highly personal, often dictated, in part, by parents' schedules. But when a child sucks to soothe herself rather than to be nourished, why not let her use what nature provided her . . . in duplicate? A thumb, after all, is right there, attached to her hand. It never disappears behind the crib bumper or into the toilet bowl. Besides, when you introduce a pacifier to a newborn, you may jeopardize breast-feeding, since babies accustomed to an artificial nipple can have trouble latching onto their mother's breast. What's more, if an infant spends too much time with a pacifier, she may nurse less frequently, causing her mother's milk supply to diminish over time.

And as if parents didn't have enough to do already, a pacifier needs to be kept clean . . . and kept track of. Usually it ends up on the floor or fuzzy at the bottom of your purse. Then there are the accessories, the little plastic boxes in which to *store* the pacifiers. There are also devices meant to keep the pacifier clipped to your baby's chest. Your infant, with the pacifier hanging by a ribbon clipped to her "onesie," looks a little like a matronly opera lover, pince-nez dangling. But the opera lover, no matter how ancient, can avail herself of her eyeglasses whenever needed. An infant who uses a pacifier has no such privilege, since she can't vacuum the device into her mouth, much less grasp it with her fingers. She has to rely on *you* to put the pacifier in her mouth and take it out—which is precisely why some parents favor it over the thumb.

That's the real problem with a pacifier: Its use is controlled by the adult, not the child. While we would never handcuff our babies to a chair, covering their mouths with duct tape, we effectively gag them every time we pop in a silicone device. We often don't know why a baby is crying, but we do know that her cries put us on edge—just as nature intended. We reach for the pacifier to *pacify our-*

selves and the other adults around us. Meanwhile, the baby who is given a pacifier every time she "fusses" comes to depend upon it, just as the baby who is held all the time requires holding . . . all the time. The merging of two needs—yours for an audible phone conversation and hers for a pacifier—can seem fortuitous, and certainly parents have a right to attend to their own lives. But you'll be cursing yourself on the airplane when you realize you forgot to pack a "binky," or when your five month old wakes up at night every time it falls from her mouth.

Then again, your baby may be waking for a more important reason: Children older than ten months of age who rely on pacifiers often suffer from a greater number of painful ear infections. Some experts believe that pacifier use can also stymie a child's communication skills. Cartoon characters who talk while "plugged"—pacifier bobbing in the mouth—may be cute, but there's nothing adorable about a toddler with delayed or unintelligible speech. More often, what many parents object to about a preschooler with a stoppered mouth is the way it looks. They find the sight of a sucking four year old unseemly or embarrassing.

Meanwhile, few adults manage to wean themselves completely of these urges, just as few of us have the "self-soothing" skills touted in baby books. Too often we turn to external aids like tobacco or alcohol to unwind, even though we know they are potentially addictive. (If we do manage to quit smoking, we often go back to sucking. . . . Only this time, we're hooked on peppermint breath mints.) Thumbs and pacifiers, too, are habit-forming, but they're habits most children abandon by the age of four. If you want to raise a resourceful child, one who knows how to help herself, let her find *inner* peace—even if, for the first few years, it seems to be lodged deep within her digit. After all, her thumb is always the right size, temperature, and flavor. And it's always available.

k.i.s.s.

toys

There's an old advertising adage—"Keep It Simple, Stupid"—that, if revised, applies to caring for a baby. Replace "Stupid" with the word "Safe." *Keep It Simple and Safe.*

That's good advice for choosing children's toys. The more active or complex the plaything, the more passive your baby will become. If by pushing a button or two, a toy goes into overdrive—spinning, lighting up, and playing "Yankee Doodle Dandy"—so will your child. Such toys drive both you and your baby to distraction. What he needs are playthings that promote concentration, not agitation. Besides, a month after buying that "cute" talking giraffe, you'll be stealing into your baby's nursery at night, screwdriver in hand, groping for the battery compartment.

Active toys excite and entertain, but they don't enrich. They're the equivalent of feeding your baby glazed donuts.

The best toys are those that can be used in myriad ways, depending on a baby's skills and imagination, as opposed to the sole way predetermined by a toy designer. After all, the designer has a single goal: to create something complicated enough to warrant the price tag.

Automated toys underestimate a child's abilities and, worse, divert him from his quest to understand nature's laws. Your tiny Newton is fascinated by the environment. He opens his hand and the teething ring falls to the floor. He does this over and over again: a lesson in gravity. He is Galileo, Einstein, and Madame Curie, all rolled into one.

It turns out that your ten month old may discover uses for a plastic colander that Julia Child never dreamed of. The kitchen is a treasure trove of simple toys for babies: cloth napkins, food storage containers, empty bottles made of plastic, measuring spoons, and rubber spatulas. You may want to move these "toys" to another part of your home or put them in your baby's play space. (The kitchen, along with the bathroom, is one of the most dangerous rooms in the house.) When selecting toys—from the kitchen or elsewhere—bear in mind that they should be lightweight so that a baby can't hurt himself or others when trying to manipulate them. The objects should be too big to be swallowed and durable enough to withstand licking and chewing. And make sure you don't need them back anytime soon.

After you've picked out a few toys, place them near your baby so he can study them and reach for the one he wants. Don't hand them to him or wave them in front of his face. But if he's unable to grasp a toy (or even a cotton scarf, which is easier for unfurling fists), he probably isn't ready to play with toys. Instead let him lie on his back and enjoy the view. Observe how he watches the ambling geometry of sunlight on the wall, outstretched hands clutching each other like two people in love. Let him feel the breeze from the open window as it lingers on his cheek like a kiss.

just (don't) say no

We all know households whose rhythms are punctuated by a single word. We may even hear that drumbeat in our own ears. If your child's every gesture seems to elicit a warning or refusal, perhaps it's you who needs to be "disciplined." Make your household safe for your child. Put away breakables. Tell *yourself* no.

Try to say "yes" to your child as often as possible. Encourage the behavior you favor. Ignore the rest. Always try to remain calm, even when your two year old throws a tantrum in the party goods store. You are your child's advocate: don't abandon or embarrass her. It's so hard, in midmeltdown, to remain compassionate, but try to give your daughter some space. Tell her you're there for her, and don't let her hurt anyone, including herself. But letting her pound on the floor, even under the horrified gaze of the shopkeeper, can work wonders. Haven't you had moments like that yourself?

Sometimes it seems our children struggle most—or we struggle with them—when we fall out of empathy with them. That's not to say your child should be placated at all costs; in fact, the healing of such breaks can bring growth. But your toddler is bound to have moments when she "loses it." She is testing you; she is testing herself. Your job is to provide boundaries, to create a structure within which she is secure. It's as if she's speeding along the Golden Gate Bridge, and you are the side rails that make her passage safe.

But you, too, may have moments when you "lose it." You have a right to your own emotions, just as you have a right, as a parent, to make mistakes. Remember you'll always get another chance to handle something better. Next time you'll be calmer, clearer, more attentive, or less afraid. Meanwhile, give *yourself* a time out—have a cup of tea or look out the window. But don't punish your child by isolating or confining *her*. You'll be amazed at how delighted you are to see your toddler again after a brief refresher. If you feel you need a break from her, she could probably use one, too. The Chinese have a saying,

"Every treasure is guarded by dragons." Every toddler is guarded by dragons, too. If you wear your own demons lightly, you teach your child resilience and self-acceptance. She learns more from a single laugh than a lifetime of rebuke.

you're only
a baby once

developmental milestones

Parents goof, screw up, and are just plain wrong more often than we'd like. Fortunately, we get second chances (and even third, fourth, and fifth chances): a chance to respond differently to a baby's 3:00 A.M. cries, a chance to apologize to a child for an angry outburst. Babies only get to be babies once. So let your baby be, and enjoy.

As a parent you shoulder a heavy enough burden as it is. Don't let developmental milestones turn into millstones. If you think you have to get down on all fours to teach your baby to crawl, ask yourself who knows more about being a baby—you at twenty, thirty, or even forty years' remove, or your seven month old? Consider how fortunate you are to have a resident expert on such matters. And remember: No prospective employer is going to look at your adult child's job application and say, "I'm sorry, only people who walked by their first birthday are being considered for the position."

Likewise, your baby is eminently qualified when it comes to play. She doesn't need you to show her how. What she *does* need is a safe space, with simple toys and someone to watch her for uninterrupted periods. There's no "right way" for her to play. If there is, you're giving her the wrong toys.

You may find that your friend's one year old browses board books while yours only chews on them. Try, however, to avoid comparing your baby to others. Different builds, temperaments, and even different styles of caregiving (no one knows the exact equation) play a role in a baby's development. Except for a small minority with real problems, all babies eventually blossom into walking, talking toddlers. We live in a society that places a premium on speed, but the acquisition of gross and fine motor skills isn't a race. Don't forget that in Aesop's fable, "The Tortoise and the Hare," the slow and steady animal triumphs. But the loser has his own spoils: He gets to take a nap.

For the first two years parents worry about what their baby *isn't* doing. Later on they worry about what their child *is* doing, or is *still* doing. Whenever your thoughts race ahead to your three year old's college graduation, stop, take a deep breath, and repeat, "My child will not be carrying a diploma in one hand . . . and sucking the thumb of the other."

Take pleasure in what your baby *can* do, and is doing, at this very moment. Instead of wishing she could roll over, marvel at the way she twists her body, like a dimpled strand of DNA, to reach a ring of plastic keys. Instead of feeling sorry for your son as he crawls *backward*, farther and farther from the ball, be grateful for this lesson on desire. Sometimes what we long for—whether it's a ball or a child who eats beets—seems to recede from us ever farther the more fervently we pursue it.

Revel in the "now." If you're always waiting for the next step, or your baby's *first* step, you're stuck in that dimly lit motel called the future. Live in the present: Your baby is waiting for you there, ready to reveal herself.

hickory, dickory, dock

Hickory, Dickory, Dock.
The mouse ran up the clock.
The clock struck one,
the mouse ran down.
Hickory, Dickory, Dock.

We all remember the nursery rhyme, with the maniacal rodent running up and down the clock. It may serve as an image of obsessive-compulsive behavior, like any rote response. But routines—like their elder cousin, ritual—serve an important function in our grown-up lives. They comfort, they clarify, they contain. The steps we take to prepare dinner help us ease the pressures of the day, just as the meal itself nourishes and refreshes. In fact, these mindless, methodical tasks—washing ourselves in the shower or making our child's sandwich for school—are sometimes the most rewarding. We know exactly what we hope to accomplish and feel certain of achieving our goal.

Children, too, are creatures of habit. Think of how often they can re-read a favorite book, wear a treasured T-shirt, or eat the same cereal from the same bowl. They like to know what's about to happen, and why, and what to expect after that. The world may seem unpredictable to them—from the constant ringing of the telephone to the scowl of a usually agreeable friend—but the routine with which they begin or end their day helps them collect their thoughts. As you ready your recalcitrant toddler for school, remind him of the tasks you'll do together: "First we'll use the toilet, then we'll get dressed, then we'll have breakfast and put on your sweater and shoes." Once he's at school, he's thrust into a mosh pit of random behavior. Your child will be grateful, as will you, that his launch was calm and within his control.

A sense of control is crucial to small children, even as their parents struggle to feel *they* are in charge. You may enlist your child to help establish a bedtime ritual. Ask him what things he most likes to do before sleep. If he has access to a computer or videos (ill-advised for very young children), don't let him use them in the hours before bed. Everything you do together should be geared toward relaxation and rest. Try to keep the routine as, well, *routine* as possible: dinner, a book, a bath, toothbrushing, and bed. Your child may need one more book before putting his head to pillow or suddenly become parched and request a glass of water. Often toddlers call us back to their side for one last, lingering hug. But don't let your child engage you in a dissertation about the moon. Allow for slight variations in routine, but be firm in the face of sheer procrastination. Sometimes a demanding toddler becomes so tired he simply can't unwind, even as his escalating orders wear our patience thin.

Announce your bedtime ritual with even the smallest child. Tell him, "Now I'm going to remove your dirty diaper; then I'll give you a bath." Similarly, break down the steps within each shift of movement or location: "I'm going to wash your hair now. You can feel the warm water on your back. Then I'll lift you out of the tub and wrap you in a cozy towel." Your child will find comfort in anticipation and may even begin to participate in the routine. Any time you supply pieces of the puzzle, whether the answer to the question, "Why is there gravity?" or clues to where his blue socks are, you make the world less unintelligible. Mystery, with its roots in the word *miracle*, is a wonderful thing for a child, but suspense—never knowing when something's going to happen—is crippling. We all know children who quite literally never seem to know whether they're coming or going; their parents haven't given them any idea when, for example, they'll be picked up from the day-care center. They spend countless, fruit-less hours unable to engage in an activity, scouring the yard for the parent who's due to arrive *whenever*. Your life may seem unpredictable to you sometimes—at any moment you could lose your wallet or your temper—but pour every ounce of energy into making life predictable for your child.

Of course, each family learns to strike its own balance, accommodating the need for flexibility and giving spon-taneity room. If you regularly come home late from work, you may push your child's bedtime back an extra half hour. If you leave for work late one morning, you may let him sleep in. Parents who work at home find the issue of predictability troubling. They like to "check in" with their child during the day, but risk disrupting his play. If you're working at home, don't keep your child in a constant state of suspense. Make exits from your office as routine as pos-sible. Tell him "Mommy will come to say 'hi' when you wake up from your nap," or, "Daddy will be giving you a snack today." As ever, your behavior is dictated by your child's needs, not by the clock. Children are mercifully free from the construct we call time. They follow an inner sense of what consumes or intrigues them. For them, the interval between preschool and dinner can stretch into eternity.

They rely on us to provide structure but not to impose strictures where none seem relevant. It's our job to give shape to their days, and nights, while allowing the time within boundaries to seem elastic, endlessly expansive. The clock itself is for that poor, benighted little mouse.

it's all relative

Imagine you're onboard a flight to Indianapolis. You've just settled in with your honeyroasted peanuts and a magazine. Suddenly, over the PA system, you can hear the copilots squabbling. "Not that button, you idiot!" one of them shouts, and your heart sinks, as if the plane were dropping from the sky.

That's what your child feels like every time you and your coparent disagree, especially when the dispute concerns her. Even the smallest infant can sense when anger mounts or silence grows poisonous. That tension is far more damaging to her than mismatched socks. Yet sometimes parents, especially mothers, rail at their mates' incompetence, or wish they could hire a baby-sitter to watch their partner watch the kids. Many fathers have a corollary complaint, that mothers are overprotective, and may bristle every time they see evidence of their partner's nervous (read: neurotic) tics. We've barely made our peace with our spouse's predilections—their charm wore off before the honeymoon was paid for—and to see these eccentricities visited on another generation can be irritating, even harrowing. As adults, we feel we're able to filter out the influence of disturbing behavior. Our children, on the other hand, do nothing but absorb and emulate.

But next time your partner screws up—forgetting to change a diaper, forgetting to discard the diaper, forgetting there *is* such a thing as a diaper—think of that passenger captive on the plane. Wait until your child is out of earshot to discuss your grievances. Remember that "It bothers me when you let her go outside without shoes" is a less contentious opener than "Everyone knows you're not supposed to . . ." or "What are you, crazy?" Your mate may have a different idea about how to dress your child or decant her juice. Don't automatically assume his methodology is wrong. Let your coparent make mistakes, just as you have both pledged to give your child the freedom to mess up, again and again. Extend to him or her the privilege to goof. And agree—again, when your child is elsewhere—on the things you won't compromise on, safety being chief among them for most parents. Set ground rules based on shared values, like banning television or sweets or making a book part of every bedtime. Agree on the big stuff, and let the smaller stuff slide.

This is one of the great challenges of parenting: believing in our partner's authority . . . and fallibility. If you've granted your child the right to be wrong, to bring home a drawing of a duck with antlers, why can't your spouse have the freedom to do things as he or she sees fit? It's as though you need to renew your vows once the stroller lands in your corridor: Recommit to seeing the best in your better half. Trust that your partner has a reason for everything she does, even when her shirt is on backwards or she's burned the toast. Remember that, in many cases, half of the baby's genetic matter belongs to your coparent. He (or she) has just as much at stake in preserving it as you do.

Yet you *will* see your partner do things you find unfathomable. Most of the time they'll do your child little harm. No toddler is irreparably damaged by not having washed her hands before a meal or by wearing his (very dirty) firefighter's pants to bed. In fact, the greatest danger a child faces is not from a hot burner or a full bath but from the possibility that her parents may part, leaving her brokenhearted and alone. You have a responsibility to protect the bond of love that prompted you to have a child, just as you must show your child that tolerance of difference is a family value and that people who love each other can disagree. Be happy that you and your mate have decided to have, adopt, or foster a child, and raise her with love. The rest will sort itself out. It's all relative. Coparenting, like copiloting, requires faith in the other's choices and in the fundamental resilience of children, who are, after all, less fragile than many relationships. It's faith, luck, and joy in each other that will keep your ship aloft—despite the occasional loss of temper and altitude.

unplugged

Television is the world's most convenient baby-sitter. It's always available, and it's cheap. When you need to return a phone call or take a shower, it's easy to plant your child in front of the tube—and console yourself with the thought that a nature program is "quality TV." But there's no reason your child can't play on the bath mat when you're in the shower; watching you through the glass is surely as interesting as watching sea turtles spawn. Everything you do—even cooking and cleaning—will fascinate your two year old. Every recipe is as unpredictable as a rocket launch.

Very young children learn by doing, by living in three dimensions. Television only offers two. What's more, the frenzied images agitate rather than stimulate, to say nothing of the violence casually observed and absorbed. Books, too, can contain troubling episodes, but your child supplies the images in his mind's eye. And you're there, as reader, to ease the impact. Why not join your kids in front of the television, too? Let them watch only as much TV as you're willing to watch with them. You may find yourself cringing and reaching for the remote. You wouldn't let a thoughtless baby-sitter pass on her values to your kids. Why let the television do it instead?

Keep in mind, too, that life isn't all entertainment— even when you're only three. Nor are children empty vessels to be filled to overflowing. For them, "down" time is "golden" time. Allowing them to become bored means letting them draw on their own resources. It means trusting them to make their own fun. A child who can reach inside himself for amusement or consolation is a child who is truly plugged in.

do as i do

"My love for you is mixed throughout my body." That's a verse from an ancient Egyptian love song. But no romantic love rivals your devotion to your newborn. Your infant consumes you, especially—literally—if you are nursing him. You give of yourself body, mind, and spirit, particularly in those first breathless, sleepless days. But you must also give *to* yourself. Give yourself a break. You have a right to your own life, even as you nurture another. By making that clear you show even the youngest child the meaning of self-worth. When you acknowledge your own limits, you encourage him not to be too hard on himself. That's the real basis for compassion and self-control.

R-E-S-P-E-C-T is more than an anthem by Aretha Franklin. It's the keystone of your relationship with your child. Respect for self, respect for others—these are values you teach your children most vividly by modeling them. We all know children who are forced to say "Please" and "Thank you" at every turn, even when they're teary or very tired. They can't get a Kleenex or a juice bottle without using the magic word. Their manners seem robotic, rote. Make sure you're not indulging your wish to have your children seem "well brought up." If you need to hear the words "Thank you," say them yourself. If you use these words appropriately with your child, he will come to volunteer them in a real context, in relation to what others ask and give. This is what he learns from you every time you really listen to him, every time you respond with authenticity. That's why your job as a parent is so consuming. You are teaching your child what it means to be human.

more k.i.s.s.es

Trees make the best mobiles. They're free and relatively easy to find. If you're lucky, there's one growing right outside your baby's window. The wind is music to its branches. So make sure cords on blinds and drapes are safely out of your baby's reach, and let the waltz of the leaves begin.

If you must buy or make a mobile (or display the one inevitably given to you at your baby shower), try hanging it somewhere other than over the crib. How would you feel trying to sleep with a rotating disco ball suspended two feet above your face?

Toys shouldn't be inescapable. Before parking your baby beneath an "infant gym," imagine working at the computer with a bead-curtain hanging between you and the screen. Every time you type, the strands of beads jump and shimmy. You would likely abandon your work in frustration, and you *can*. *You* can get up and walk away . . . but your four month old can't. "Activity bars" that dangle in front of a baby's face in the stroller or car seat trap your baby into paying attention to them. He might prefer to look at a passing dog or examine his foot. If given the freedom to lie flat on their backs and explore, babies are naturally active. They don't need personal trainers.

Similarly, a baby's sleep space should never be cluttered with hard or noisy toys. Let it be a calm, safe environment suitable for . . . sleep. One or two soft items are usually sufficient: a cotton diaper or cloth, a shirt redolent of Mom or Dad, or a small, washable stuffed animal.

If your baby is fussy or having difficulty napping, try the greatest possible "pacifier," the outdoors. Nature is the antidote to so many ills—an adult's office worries as well as a two month old's indigestion. The outdoors has the miraculous power to awaken and still something in all of us, resuscitating the work-weary and quieting little ones. As Ralph Waldo Emerson wrote: "Adopt the pace of nature. Her secret is patience." Let that be your secret, too.

If you don't have a yard, find a park or patch of grass near your home. Go there with your baby and place him on a blanket beneath a tree. As adults, we spend so much time in life looking ahead. Take a moment to lie down next to him and look up. Just look up.

brain aerobics

offering choices

New parents, especially breast-feeding moms, complain of not being able to think straight. But minding a baby doesn't mean losing your mind. Sleep deprivation, a surge of hormones, and temporary loss of contact with the outside world can make even the most resourceful parent feel her brain has gone belly up.

Your three month old may have more synapses than you do, but the latest neuroscience reveals that cognitive development occurs throughout life—even in the early months of parenting. In other words, you *can* teach an old dog new tricks. The tricks may include putting a drop of breast milk in your newborn's nose to clear a head cold, or placing a damp diaper briefly in the microwave and then on your breast to soothe the breast if it becomes inflamed. But the most hard-won insights come from careful observation of your infant. Think of it as "field work." Only, unlike Jane Goodall, who lived among the chimpanzees in Tanzania, you don't have to crawl on your belly through vines to catch your subject in her natural state. She's lying there in the crib next to your bed, probably even studying you, too.

Goodall said that the aspect of her research she savored most was waking up and asking herself, "What am I going to see today?" Studying your baby will yield valuable clues about how to care for her and yourself. Is she really hungry, or is that the whimpering sound she makes when sleepy? Consider your task "Applied Research." When you're finally able to understand her "calls, postures and gestures," as Goodall referred to them, you'll know when to put her down for a nap . . . and grab a little shut-eye yourself.

You'll need your rest, because the hardest work is yet to come. By the time your child is a year old, get ready for Brain Aerobics. Toddlers can be quick on their feet, and keeping yours safe—and engaged in shared tasks like diapering, bathing, and eating—requires that you be quick-witted. If you offer your child choices (limit them to two until she's of preschool age) and allow her to voice an opinion, her involvement will be greater and the experience more enjoyable for you both. Coming up with *real* choices, as well as imaginative ways to tell your child "No," will keep your mind limber.

If you're alone with your two year old and need to go to the market, don't ask, "Would Hallie like to go with Mommy to the store?" What if she says, "No"? She can't stay home by herself, after all. Would you offer your dinner guests raspberry tarts for dessert, knowing full well you haven't any? When soliciting your child's input, take her preferences into account, but don't derail your plans: "Would you like to go to the store *before* or *after* lunch?"

If you shrill "No!" or "Careful!" every time your baby looks as though she may bump her head, you risk becoming the proverbial broken record. You'll bore yourself, she'll tune you out, and, worst of all, you'll have robbed these words of their power. The day your child's *truly* in danger—about to run into the street—what will you say to protect her? If you repeat the same cautionary phrases over and over, your only recourse for getting her attention will be to shout, leaving you hoarse and frustrated.

Resistance exercises aren't just for the body. Fight against familiar or reflexive responses by finding shorthand descriptions specific to each danger. If you see your baby across the room crawling under a low table, try saying, "The table is above your head." If she's about to stand up, it's just as easy to say, "Table," while patting your head as it is to shriek, "Watch out!" Similarly, if your child is playing in the tub, you may want to let her know, "The faucet is behind you," while placing your hand between her back and the sharp-edged spout. How much detail you use will depend on your child's level of understanding and the urgency of the situation. If you've given the full explanation once or twice already—"You're close to the edge of the bed; the edge is the place where you can fall and hurt yourself"—and you're standing nearby, an abbreviated version will suffice. "The edge," you remind her, running your fingers the length of the peril. Trust her to know exactly what you mean.

Translating negative commands into positive instructions is another brain buster. Instead of saying, "Don't pour your milk on the floor," try, "The milk needs to stay in the cup or in your mouth." After you've told your child more than once that it's not safe to stand on the chair, pat the seat and remind her, "This is made for holding bottoms." If that doesn't work, a spoonful of silliness may make the discipline go down: "At the dinner table only chairs use their legs!"

Keeping a sense of humor (or developing one) is like weight training for parents. It gives you the strength to set limits and makes abiding by them less onerous for your child. But no matter how light-hearted or patient you are, there will be times when your child seems incapable of doing what you say. When your little one misbehaves, it's okay if you sometimes lose your cool, but *she* should never lose face. Teaching your child the consequences of her actions while treating her with respect—there is no greater test of stamina than this.

food fight

You've put on the rabbit ears and hopped around the kitchen. You've sung every verse you can remember to "Food, Glorious Food." But your baby looks as grim and disapproving as a society matron at a Megadeth concert. No matter what you do, he won't eat.

Stop trying. Children, especially those who are newly masters of their universe, are notoriously picky. Just because he'll put anything in his mouth, from parts of your new blender to the droppings of a sycamore tree, doesn't mean he'll consume the diced carrots on the tray of his high chair. Maybe the high chair itself is the problem. True, we all were made to sit in high chairs as children, even as we *weren't* secured in car seats when traveling. But children should be confined only when safety is at issue, not for the sake of convenience or cleanliness. Toddlers get messy when learning to eat, and the noodles plastering

50

their hair . . . and their clothes . . . and the wall behind them . . . are a sign that they're making a go of it.

High chairs may contain the mess, but they also constrain your child. He has little to do, once he's stopped eating, other than to squirm or drop his spoon. Once he's dropped his spoon, or thrown the diced carrots, or howled, and you've released him for what seems like the millionth time, you might consider getting an adjustable chair. Such a chair allows your child to sit "high" at the dinner table or low enough to excuse himself when he's tired of eating or feels full. A tray on the floor, or a child-sized table for snacks, also gives your child the sense of autonomy that's as crucial as any multivitamin. If he is able to move more freely, he might even consider chowing down, and you may just trade your toddler's immobility for the pleasure of seeing him eat. But don't let him wander away while munching or stroll through the house with snacks. Eating is a focused activity; it should be done sitting down.

Babies unable to sit on their own should never be confined to a high chair or other contraption for eating. During a meal, the place for them is on your lap. Hold your baby firmly, at an angle, so you can see his mouth and follow his cues. Let him tell you when he's hungry, by crying or by opening his mouth to signal readiness for another bite.

Don't prop up a bottle, allowing your infant to receive milk as if from an IV drip. You're not trying to "stabilize" a patient in the ICU; you're trying to nourish an infant, and nourishment comes from human contact as well as from a bottle. When you position a bottle on top of pillows or hand it off like a baton, you send the message that the act of feeding is inconvenient or of little consequence. A newborn can see only as far as the face poised above him: Remember that he is watching you, even as you are watching him. If you're short on time, cancel plans to take him for an afternoon encounter with the cocker spaniel down the street, but never rush through a feeding. This is the ultimate "quality" time.

One way to *save* time is to stop pureeing fruits and vegetables for your finicky eater once he cuts some teeth. Pediatricians warn against giving whole grapes or pieces of hot dog to a child under the age of one, but otherwise, dice whatever unseasoned food you're eating into small pieces and serve it up. The sooner your child learns to eat what you eat, the more compatible he'll be with the family's meal routines, and the more money you'll save on baby food. He'll be readier, too, to accompany you to your favorite restaurant.

Forewarned is forearmed at your local bistro. Tell even the smallest child what the rules are; if things go badly, don't hesitate to leave, even if you have to take the food you've already ordered "to go." Many parents travel with a box of straws, to make beverages accessible. Others always carry a plastic container of a favorite food, like cereal, from home. The dishes you order should be prepared simply, without spices. Let sauce, on the side, be your SOS. New eaters can also dip green beans into a bowl of grated Parmesan cheese for hours—or at least, for the twenty minutes it takes grown-ups to wolf down their meal.

Flavored yogurt is another favorite of the pint-sized connoisseur, ideal for dipping a strawberry or slice of honeydew. For a while, anyway, your toddler may think of this as dessert. "Real" dessert should be saved for special occasions. It's not an inalienable right. Try not to exoticize sweets by forbidding your child to taste them; once he is older and eating snacks at friends' houses, he may be swallowed whole by the cookie jar. But a child who is invited to experiment with tastes may choose cantaloupe over a cupcake, if he hasn't been conditioned to prefer a tricked-up sweetness to what's juicy and fresh.

Children are by nature explorers, and they take to unlikely foods as readily as Margaret Mead took to the customs of the island of Ta'u. Let your child pursue his passions, and resist waging war over every uneaten pea. You will have won a huge battle, for yourself and your child, if you do.

being there

slowing down and doing less

"Slow down, you move too fast. You got to make the morning last." Many of us found this '60's anthem, by Simon and Garfunkel, annoying. It didn't . . . well, it didn't *move* enough. We wanted something more syncopated, more agitated. Now that we're parents, our preferences haven't changed.

Many new parents, especially if they're first-time parents at an older age, come from a fast-paced, career-oriented world. They're used to doing too much—crawling the web while talking on the phone and scarfing down a burrito—and, in fact, they pride themselves on it; it's the closest they get to a "natural" high. But new parents have a new job, a *slow* job, with real challenges, especially for those who are leisure impaired. They need to learn how to be with their baby and how to let their baby be.

For parents who aren't used to doing just *one* thing,

doing *nothing* can be the hardest job of all. Whenever their infant cries, they rush to pick him up, jiggling him frantically, while winding up the musical toy that swings, annoyingly, above his crib. Their rapid response time could rival any paramedic's. They turn even a routine flare-up into a three-alarm fire. But needless to say, babies don't respond well to these frenzied efforts. In fact, when newborns are jostled in a misguided effort to recreate the motion of the womb, they may not get it: Having been much more recently in the womb, they're probably better equipped to re-create its rhythm than we are. But new parents always feel they need to do something, to *be* something, to *help*. Allowing your infant to cry, even for an extra ten seconds, while you move *slowly* toward him *is* helpful. It gives him additional time to soothe himself, and offers you a chance to reflect on what he's feeling and respond appropriately.

For starters, you don't need to scream, "I'M COMING!" *He's* not going anywhere. Imagine what he sees as you rush toward him, arms flapping, mouth agape. That's not going to calm anybody down. Remember, as you struggle to turn off the sirens and flashing lights, that you want your child to associate you with constancy, not velocity. This moment, like much of parenting, is all about being there . . . not about being there *fast*.

Similarly, you don't want to rush your baby when

you're dressing or bathing him, especially if he doesn't enjoy these tasks. He won't like them more because you're rushing; in fact, he may get the message that you don't like them much yourself. Better to find ways to simplify a job, like choosing clothing with fewer snaps or a "onesie" that you don't need to shove over his head. Or, if he's genuinely hydrophobic, sponge bathe him or let the bath go for the night. Talking him through a job also helps allay some of the unpleasantness. He'll find the sound of your voice calming and will come to understand your words and know when the job is almost finished. But try never to cajole or coerce him; even the tiniest child will sense your insincerity. Would you rather have a clean baby, or one who trusts you to hear and see him, dirt and all?

What children, especially the youngest children, want more of is *less*: less commotion, less activity. As they age, they will still prefer doing "nothing" to most scheduled activities. Sure, they love being taken to the beach or to a birthday party; but most of the time, they're happiest just hanging out. Ask your four year old, "Wanna go to the market with me, and then we'll mail this package at the post office? Then we can drop Daddy's watch at the repair shop." Most of the time, a resounding silence will be his response. You may try to tempt him with a stop at the bakery (even though you know you shouldn't). The real reward for a child is just to stay home.

For the same reason, small children don't need to attend multiple classes so they can learn to fence or sculpt even before they can spell their name. Your four year old will create worlds if left to his own devices, knowing an adult's nearby to help fasten a crown or rebuild a moat. If you do feel the need to get him involved in an organized activity—and sometimes reticent children do need to "mix it up" with other kids—try to pick just one class and let your child help choose. But nothing compares to the elaborate, taxing, and fulfilling games your child can create . . . at home. And the child who learns to entertain himself, like the baby who masters the art of self-soothing, will be developing lifelong skills.

But we, parents who do too much, insist it's in our children's best interests to be "busy" and "learning" all the time. We shuttle them from football practice to art class so they can learn about discipline and cooperation, but mostly what they learn is how much they hate being in the car. As children grow, their schedules can seem ever more constricting: Older children are frequently penalized for missing athletic practices or discouraged from taking family vacations during spring break. Coaches, whose budgets are often based on their team's "success," aren't going to help parents scale back on these commitments. Parents must insist on it themselves.

Doing so means also cutting back on our own commitments, simplifying our social calendar, and learning to say no. If you throw away your daily planner, your child may jettison his, and teachers do report seeing first graders carrying daily planners among their books. Parents must allow tarry time for a small child and also for the teenager he will become. Older kids can always find ways to *avoid* being with their parents. (We did when we were young.) But that gap can have deadly consequences: Witness recent acts of violence among teenagers whose parents had surrendered them to the influence of the media and their peers. Older children need you to *be there* for them, not just physically but emotionally, and they're likelier to talk to a parent who's around and open to them. Parenting from the sidelines, even if you fanatically attend every one of your daughter's soccer matches, isn't the same as actually being *with* your child.

The idea of spending time as a family can seem corny or dated—remember puzzle night?—but you can design outings that reflect your child's interests, like going to a mask-making day at your local museum or to a state fair. Accustom him early on to your influence, but also to your willingness to create distance, to allow privacy. Infants, toddlers, and teenagers share an important requirement: that parents be available but respectful, too. They want to know you are there, but not *everywhere*. Respect their need for secrets, for hiding places, for trust.

Giving a child space—another '60s concept—can be very liberating for a parent because it also allows you some breathing room. You, too, may be happier if your days don't feel so constricted. No one needs to be on every school committee. Try to pace yourself. Remember that some of the most beautiful parts of a canvas are the parts that remain unpainted, unresolved. Let your child's self-portrait be open to the sunlight, dappled with possibilities. Take your cues from another '60s anthem: Let him be.

body language

"I am large, I contain multitudes," Walt Whitman wrote, but he wasn't talking about being pregnant. Watching our bellies expand, many women can't help but wonder, *Will my body ever be the same?* The worst part is the girl at the checkout counter who asks when you're due . . . three months after you've brought your baby home. Remember: It takes nine months of pregnancy to put the weight on, and at least nine months to take it off. If you plan to breast-feed until your child turns one (as recommended by the American Academy of Pediatrics), you may discover that those last pounds linger until you wean. Even if the scale does register familiar numbers, you may still feel out of shape. Depending on what kind of wheels your baby has, you can walk or jog with her, but getting to the gym is out of the question for many new moms. Few health clubs offer child care, and most of us don't have the means to hire a baby-sitter while we jazzercize.

The good news is that your baby will soon have you on the run: Once your child begins to crawl, you can kiss the couch good-bye. Bellowing prohibitions from your La-Z-Boy is not a terribly effective way of stopping a ten month old from tugging on a lamp cord. If you regret never studying French, now is your chance to get off your *derrière* and learn a second language: body language. When your child's doing something dangerous or destructive, you need to get up, cross the room, squat down to her level, establish eye contact, and explain, in as calm a voice as you can muster, what behavior is safe and acceptable. Tell her, "I don't want you to touch the cord. If you pull it, the lamp may fall. I don't want you to get hurt or the lamp to break." If she continues to be curious or cannot control herself, place your hand or even your whole body between her and the potential threat. Say something as simple as, "I can't let you touch the cord." Caring for a toddler is a little like playing basketball: A tight defense is the best way to block a shot. But unlike in sports, you're not trying to prevent the offense from scoring; you're trying to teach your child limits that she'll internalize to keep her safe.

If your toddler charges toward the swimming pool, and you react by picking him up and carrying him back to the toys on the grass, he is likely to think it's a game and insist on playing it over and over again. You can cart him away ten times without missing the punch line of your friend's joke, but what you'll miss is a chance to discipline your child. Don't forget, "discipline" and "disciple" come from the same root; "to discipline" doesn't mean *to punish*, but *to teach*. Think of your eighteen month old as your disciple. If you want him to become a follower, a true believer, the place to convert him is at the water's edge. The more fully he understands your teachings, the simpler parenting will be.

When your sixteen month old is batting at the blossoms of a potted plant or pulling off petals, place your hand between him and the plant, while letting him know what he may and may not do. "Touch the flowers gently like this, with an open hand. The plant is a living thing. I don't want you to hit it. When you do that all the petals fall off and we won't have beautiful flowers to enjoy. Would you like to cut one together and put it in a vase?" You may have to repeat this interaction five or six times . . . a day, for several days. If you grow tired of intervening, remove the plant for the remainder of the day, but don't remove your baby. You don't want to send a message that obstacles are to be avoided. Stay and work out a solution. When the going gets tough, the tough *don't* go anywhere.

This kind of proactive parenting will get your heart rate up, while keeping your blood pressure down. For a head-to-toe workout, follow this simple but challenging routine: Stretch by finding descriptive and positive alternatives to the word no, do as many repetitions of choice offering as you can (make the choices count!), and move your hips, not just your lips, when instructing your toddler. If you're caring for a small child, think of yourself as an athlete-in-training. Parenting, after all, is the ultimate long-distance event.

be a believer

Some people believe in fairies. Others swear by the Nasdaq. Still others think the patter between talk show hosts and their guests is unscripted, genuine. We all have our beliefs and we cling to them fiercely, in the face of disillusion, and of the dissolution of the past century, during which nations crumbled and turned inward, clan against clan.

New parents are often among the most ingenuous because they have witnessed or been the beneficiaries of a miracle. The tiny, mewling creature thrust into your arms seems more perfect than perfection, even if his ears stick out or her hair looks like a Mohawk. We all remember the sensation of taking our baby home, as our spouse or friend pulls up to the hospital in a car, or helps us into a cab. We glance around us, incredulous, wondering, "Where is the grown-up accompanying us? How can people trust us to care for this creature *ourselves*?"

But they do, and gradually, through trial and error (and more error), we persevere. Despite our mishaps, our children thrive, even when we do the unthinkable, like putting a Band-Aid on an infant's finger, only to have it disappear down her throat. The process of child rearing can make a believer out of anyone: somehow the world seems charmed, and we have never felt so blessed. But even the sunniest newborn, when her sleeping patterns change, can try our patience; the minute our children "fail" us, we may begin to scrutinize them. Everyone else's four month old is smiling or sucking contentedly. No one else's newborn has cradle cap. The infant acne that mars a thousand photos can seem like a biblical plague and, because we're sleep deprived, it all feels personal. And these afflictions are nothing compared to the despair a parent feels at a four year old's struggles in school or her inability to bond with anyone on the playground. Our faith in our child's perfection can falter, especially if the kid next to her seems poised and self-confident. Why isn't our child better? Why is she doing this to *us*?

Nothing is more deadening to a child than a parent's skepticism; it spreads like toxic waste, poisoning everything in its path. The truth is, children who are trusted tend to fulfill or exceed their parents' expectations, just as colleges with honor codes report fewer instances of cheating on tests. But faith of any kind is never for the fainthearted. It takes practice and disappointment on both sides. Don't wait until you're handing your teenager the car keys to find out what his values are. The child you want to talk to about condoms is the child you talked to about crayons. Start, for example, when your infant first begins waking at night. Trust that he's genuinely hungry or otherwise needy, not that he's irritable or a "bad" sleeper. Many of us have over-heard parents referring to their child as a "demon seed." How does it serve anyone, parent or child, to be counted upon to be *bad*?

Ironically, we must help our children *learn* to fail us. It's a dirty job, if ever there was one, but essential to our child's growth. When children screw up—misbehaving in a restau-rant, for example, and forcing a noisy exodus after our order has been placed—they see the consequences of being dis-ruptive or impatient. Parents, too, learn to be consistent, never threatening to do things (leave a restaurant after the order is placed?) they don't really intend to do. Janusz Kor-czak, the head of a Jewish orphanage during the fiercest years of Nazi rule, created a children's bill of rights, and among its precepts was a child's right to fail. Startlingly, he also insisted on the following proposal: His charges must be allowed one lie, one deception, or theft. Why one?

One lie, and the havoc that ensues, may be all many children need to think twice about lying next time. Experience is a most reliable tutor; many of us had to sneak only one cigarette—and gag—before swearing off tobacco forever, realizing, as our parents had warned us, that it would "make us sick." (Sometimes, even *our* parents were right about things.) Yet it's important not to anticipate your children's failure, any more than you would assume they've been injured every time they fall. The little girl who's constantly introduced as "shy" may find herself tongue-tied and begin to withdraw, just as the little boy who is "aggressive" will explode, as if on demand. The key is to describe your child's behavior in a neutral, respectful way, if you must comment at all: "My daughter likes to take a moment to observe when she first enters a situation" of the child who's cautious, or "He needs a little space when he's settling in" of the child who grabs other children's toys. Plan for your child's success by sitting with her in a strange situation while she warms up, or bringing several of his toys from home to ease him into a shared space. The natural grace and decency of children will often carry the day, if we trust them to behave appropriately.

Even the children in Korczak's orphanage knew how to rise to the occasion. In fact, they held the banner of their orphanage aloft as they were led to the death trains. So irresistible was the image of their bravery—the flag fluttering above their heads—that the Nazi soldiers saluted instinctively. Korczak taught his charges to value hope above fear and to embrace death with self-possession, even poise. Blessedly, your children's struggles will be of magnitudes that are worlds smaller. But the courage you instill in them can make them incandescent.

baby steps

When children are acquiring a new skill—like walking or using the toilet—they often begin by taking giant strides. The next day they may resort to what's familiar and has worked for them in the past: The toddler who peed in the potty yesterday insists on doing so in his diaper today. Disappointed parents wonder if yesterday's "success" was due to "beginner's luck," or to sheer novelty. They may even worry that—horrors—their child is "regressing," whatever that means. In fact, he's learning the way most of us did in our early years (and sometimes still do): taking two steps forward and one step back. Forget about the learning curve; it's more like the cha-cha-cha.

Whatever you call these steps, *you* are your child's dance partner, but make sure *he's* the one who leads. When your baby or toddler is striving to accomplish something, your role is to follow his cues. The nine month old who wants to crawl downstairs head first doesn't need to be taught the "safe" way to go down, which is supposedly on his bottom. Let him practice *his* way on a small set of two or three stairs if you can. If not, simply sit two steps below and "spot" him, and be sure to gate off the stairs when you're unavailable. In no time, of his own accord, he'll switch to going down feet first, facing the steps—as if climbing down a ladder. And he'll have learned to do so on his own.

Likewise, when your toddler is straining to reach a toy on the table, don't hand it to him. Try moving it an inch or two closer instead. Ask yourself, "Why do I feel I need to help? What matters more, my child's desire for the toy or the lesson that he can meet his own needs?"

Before long he'll abandon his teething ring to chew on meatier matters: "Why is the snow white?" or "Why can't people fly?" When your child begins the dizzying waltz of the "whys," you may feel like stepping on his feet just to slow him down. Try to echo his movements instead. Respond to his questions with questions of your own: "Why *is* the snow white?" "What would it be like to fly? Where would *you* go?" You may find your child's answers more fascinating than any Fox Mulder would supply.

Even pleas for help are sometimes best met by a question. Your child may ask, "Can you turn on the light in the bathroom? I can't reach it." Try saying, "Oh, that's right. What can you bring to stand on so you *can* reach it? Do you think your stool might work?" If you don't turn on the light yourself, it's not because you're a lazy parent, it's because you want your child to learn to solve problems on his own. In fact, it's much more demanding to interact with your child this way, but also more rewarding . . . for both of you. Remember, the worst thing you can do for those you love is something they could and should do for themselves.

These lessons are, of course, tough to recall in the middle of a crisis, especially if you've been up three nights in a row. When we wake in the middle of the night, most us are able to fall back to sleep—eventually. Your baby, too, will learn how to do this if you give him a chance. That doesn't mean you should ignore his cries, especially if you think he might be hungry or sick. Rather, respond by doing a little *less* than you might otherwise, and allow your baby to do *more*. If, at the first whimper, you speed to his side and airlift him out of the crib to nurse or rock him, you'll have used up all your resources and denied him the chance to draw on his own strengths. Remember, your child's not a plane crash survivor in the Andes. He's a sleepy baby. So leave some tricks in your bag.

. . .

Start by speaking to him from the doorway ("I hear you crying. It's still dark. I want you to go back to sleep. Good night."), and then return to your room. If he continues to cry, you may need to up the ante a bit: Kneel beside his crib and touch him through the bars, while speaking soothingly. If you have to take him out of the crib, don't feel that either one of you has failed. You must demonstrate the steps to sleep in as low-key and graceful a manner as you can . . . at 3:00 A.M. Then try—easier said than done—to fall back to sleep yourself.

Dancing isn't the only diversion involving steps. Some of us may recall playing "Mother, may I?" when we were little. This is a game in which a "parent" stands at the finish line, giving instructions like "Take two giant steps forward," or "Take one baby step backward." The child who forgets to ask, "Mother, may I?" before proceeding is sent back to the starting line. Every time you do things *for* your child because it's faster or because you can't bear to see him struggle, you send him back to the starting line defeated. Rushing to his assistance may make *you* feel competent—like a good parent—but it can have the opposite effect on your child by creating a sense of inadequacy. Next time you're helping out, remember to take baby steps. Your child will feel like a giant if you do.

the apple and
the tree

They say the apple doesn't fall far from the tree. But sometimes what falls from the tree isn't an apple at all. It may be a pear or a plum or a hippopotamus, meaning that your offspring, your fruit, may surprise you by its very nature. It's not just that your daughter has violet eyes when everyone in the family for generations has had brown, or that your son loves to build airplanes out of blocks when you aspire for him to be the next Tiger Woods. It's that your child's temperament and inclinations and preferences are entirely unpredictable, almost from the moment he or she emerges and is placed in your arms. You know that your newborn will be hungry and sleepy—almost nothing else can be counted on.

New parents love to point out the cleft in a chin that resembles Uncle Rocky's, or the funny way a child has of gesturing or screwing up her eyes. We look for resemblance, partly for the pleasure of seeing ourselves in someone else, partly for reassurance when things go poorly. ("Well, my father has a temper, too.") But our children, whether biological or not, are always *other*, and the sooner we accept that, the easier our passage with them will be. They do not belong to us, and we cannot read in them our likeness, no matter how hard we try.

Which means we have to give them the freedom to write their own story, almost from the moment we remove the tiny hospital bracelet from their wrist. The blanket they come home in may be the last clothing choice we feel we can stand behind. (We may feel differently when, torn to tatters, it reappears three years later as a cape.) But when your four year old emerges from her closet dressed like a cross between a clown and a cross-dresser, try not to react too strongly. Say, "Wow, there's a lot going on in that outfit," rather than, "Where's the party dress Aunt Janey bought you? Go back and put that on!" It may be that Aunt Janey is about to descend on you for a visit, in which case you may want to ease your child into the dress at some point. But unless it's absolutely crucial, it's better to reserve judgment and allow your child just to be. Most people you meet, or at least most parents, will remember having had similar clothing crises. They're not weighing your fitness as a parent based on your child's outfit; chances are, they're too busy studying the shrieking combination of plaids and stripes, or the fairy wings bulging beneath the cardigan. If you remove yourself from the picture, you may find you're not the center of attention at all.

The key to solidarity in such moments is to remember that your child exists apart from you. You don't have to smile indulgently at her in front of others and say, "She chose that outfit herself." They can *tell*. Better just to support her show of individuality. You don't have to explain her to the world. Choices in food and clothing are rarely worth battling about and not because you may feel you'll never win. Far better to control the battlefield by getting rid of clothes that fit poorly or foods you don't think are nutritious enough. Learn to trust your child so that she can begin to trust herself. She may like the bath water so frigid you expect to see ice cubes floating in it or refuse to wear a sweater even as her teeth chatter and her eyes stream. Just because you're cold doesn't mean that your four year old is, or if she is, she may not be bothered by it. *You* are.

Sometimes we imagine our children are cold or hungry, not just because *we* would be in the same circumstance, but because we're used to feeling cold when we get depressed or solving problems by eating too much or eating the wrong foods. Again, we assume our child resembles us. She may not. You need to be true to yourself: If you're hungry, eat, but let your child go play if she's not interested in her food. Say, "We're having dinner now. If you don't want to eat, feel free to play with your toys. But dinner will be over soon; then I'll be putting away the food." You don't have to run an all-night diner. You're allowed to have your own life, too. But so is your child, and the sooner you free her, the fewer struggles you'll have with her.

If you're always telling your child how to feel, she won't learn to trust her own sensations, her inner thermometer. She knows what a coat is for and will avail herself of it when needed. But meanwhile she may be off in her own world, imagining she's on a space shuttle or in a bat cave. If you tune into her, you'll learn worlds about how her imagination works. You'll see your child with new eyes and, if you create some distance, may even save yourself some emotional wear and tear. As a parent, you have enough to do without trying to worm your way into your child's mind and heart. Tend to your own garden and let your pear or plum—or hippopotamus—ripen or flourish as it will.

walking the
walk

learning to walk

 You'd like to forget "the Macarena," and you can dimly recall "the Hustle," but have you ever done "the Caveman Shuffle"? This dance requires a grown-up to lumber behind a wobbly toddler, hunching over him to hold his tiny, raised hands. It's hard to say who looks more Neanderthal: the barely bipedal baby or the stooped parent. But it's safe to bet this couple won't win any ballroom prizes.

Like riding a bike, walking takes balance. There's no reason, however, that you should strain your back acting as your child's training wheels. That's what his arms and hands are for. Unlike tightrope walkers at the circus, your teetering baby doesn't need a net. If his arms and hands are free, he'll use them to protect himself in a spill. Provided he's on flat ground, he doesn't have far to fall.

In walking, as in life, learning to fall and fail are important lessons. Confucius said, "Our greatest achievement is not in never falling but in rising every time we fall." When your baby *does* take a tumble, avoid grimacing or gasping. Also, don't assume you have to rescue him or whisk him back to his feet. Often children are more upset by the look on our face and the urgency of our response than by any injury. When he does fall—as he inevitably will—walk slowly toward him, crouch beside him and calmly describe what you think happened. Ask, with extended arms, if he needs your help.

He probably doesn't, any more than a crawling baby needs to be hurried through this development stage. Yet many parents are uncomfortable seeing their babies on all fours, getting "down and dirty." They consider crawling a necessary evil. After all, crawling babies can be downright inconvenient, especially when traveling. Try skulking behind an eight month old during the in-flight movie, while he devours leftovers from the aisle and narrowly escapes the beverage cart. It's no wonder parents are eager for their children to join the ranks of the ambulatory. (What's more, few can resist the sight of those miniature hiking boots dangling in the storefront window at the mall.) But remember, the best support for your child's feet is the ground beneath them. Stiff-soled shoes will keep his feet clean, but they'll also keep him from really feeling the floor. At the beginning, that's just as important as putting one foot in front of the other.

Babies who learn to walk on their own, at their own pace—cruising from chair to sofa, then standing solo before finally launching forth—tend to move more gracefully and fall less often. If you're always offering a "helping hand," your baby may come to rely on it and take longer to gain his balance. Don't worry. There will be plenty of occasions to hold your child's hand: in a crowded market, crossing the street, going down an especially steep staircase, or just because you feel like it. You are, after all, two people in love.

Your baby may take his first steps as early as nine months (or as late as fifteen months), but chances are he'll begin walking around the time he turns a year old. His first steps will mark the end of "babyhood" and the beginning of his journey toward independence. Like adolescent aborigines who venture into the wilderness alone as a rite of passage, your child is embarking on a "walkabout." Perhaps that's why walking is such a momentous milestone, commemorated in every baby book and prompting phone calls to family and friends. Go ahead, celebrate. Everybody knows parents like to boast. But babies are born doers—executives with goals and vision—whose support staff sometimes gets in the way. You may talk the talk, but be sure it's your baby who's walking the walk . . . on his own.

octopus mom

There is a kind of Australian spider that lays her eggs, then lives barely long enough to see her offspring mature. She nestles among them and begins to decompose, becoming an edible blob they can consume as they begin life. Most mothers aren't capable of such sacrifice, nor should they be, although they sometimes feel they are melting into their sweatpants, spit-up stuck to their shirt. But becoming a parent means giving up a lot, including things you didn't think you could live without: an impromptu date with your spouse, a chance to finish that office memo uninterrupted, even the pleasure of a hot shower sometime before dusk settles in.

Being a new parent is a great excuse to simplify, to clarify one's priorities, to leave phone calls unreturned and dishes unwashed. New parents need to trust others to do things (like going to the bank) and will even, although it seems unthinkable, have to find someone to care for their infant when a trip to the dentist cannot be postponed another day. You need to say yes to the friend or relative who keeps offering to pick up groceries for you and no to the people who need your help with a fund-raiser. For working mothers, this can be especially difficult, even if you're taking a federally mandated parenting leave. Coworkers will call "just to ask a question" and keep you on the phone for hours complaining about your boss, or fax you a document "for you to look over when you get a chance." If you've agreed to the disruption by assuring your coworkers that you'll always "be available," you need to let them know *when* you're available. Structure your time at home. Gently insist that all calls be placed in the late morning, when your infant is napping or when your mother comes in to watch him. Most important, if you know you'll be called away for several hours, make sure to spend several hours of "quality time" with your child. That means time spent with your child doing whatever he or she requires, nursing or playing or just cuddling together on the floor. Such time exists—and counts—even with the smallest infant. In fact, your child may grow needier as she grows older, and will be more disruptive, if you haven't put in this time.

But magazine articles for mothers who've worked, or

who will return to work soon, tend to exploit our capacity for organization, our sense of responsibility . . . and our guilt. They encourage women to think we can have it all, or at least micromanage it all. In effect you'll be giving your child 0 percent of your attention 100 percent of the time. Advice about "multitasking" can seem almost ludicrous as you imagine breast-feeding your infant while scrubbing the floor and blow-drying your hair. Parenting is about focus, about giving your infant undivided attention without resentment or distraction—even if it's only for ten minutes a day. It's about learning that almost everything, except your child, can wait.

Remember, no one is scrutinizing the crumbs on your kitchen floor. No one cares if you haven't colored your roots or sent your coworker a birthday card. We live in a fractured, high-speed world, in which time to concentrate is as endangered as the wild mandrill. Children, especially, are the unwilling targets of relentless stimuli. If you want your child to master the skills needed for essential tasks— from self-soothing to learning to read—you want to model for her the ability to do one thing well, wholeheartedly.

Soon enough you will not be able to avoid doing multiple tasks simultaneously. You'll be signaling for a right turn while reaching into the backseat to hand your toddler a bottle, or cleaning up paints even as you supervise her trip to the kitchen with her self-portrait dripping on the floor. You'll be "octopus mom." But there's a difference between doing too much—or attempting too many things too soon—and doing the myriad tasks we do as caregivers. If you're the one at home with your baby, try not to cringe when someone asks, "What have you been doing all day?" You've been doing something very important: being. Being with your baby.

Soon you'll be back at work and perhaps, even sooner, your child will be able to entertain herself. But for now your baby needs you. Try to put other parts of your life on hold. You may even discover how understanding the world is when you explain that you have an infant at home. You don't have to liquefy into an edible blob for her to consume. But there *are* things only you can give her. The world can wait.

in loco parentis

f i n d i n g   a   c a r e g i v e r

It's incredible, unfathomable . . . and unavoidable. You need to leave your infant with a caregiver. Maybe it's time to go back to work, and so you must give up long, lovely days helping your five month old find his toes. Or maybe you just have a toothache that can't wait. Whatever the reason, there comes a time when you'll need to resume your grown-up life, which means more than just getting a haircut and a good night's sleep. It means going out into the world without the crucial, tiny being who has redefined your existence—and (mercifully) without his diaper bag, car seat, bottles, and smattering of toys.

Most parents dread that first time away because they can't believe their infant will survive, let alone thrive, without them. They make endless lists of emergency numbers for the caregiver (which is especially insulting if the person you're leaving your baby with is Dad). New parents worry about *everything*—the angle of the car seat, the smell of the newly painted crib—but one particularly groundless fear is that they will never endure being away from their child. In fact, it's a good thing—for you and for your infant—to have some time apart. It'll only make your tender feelings stronger, and his, too. What's more, you'll be reminded of a whole world out there, of people and cars and movies that have opened in the last few months. In truth, it's a world you may have missed more than you care to admit.

New parents look at those who have a regular "date night" the way expectant parents view the film shown at the last Lamaze class. The people on-screen—having birthed a baby, cuddling and crying—seem to have accomplished something unimaginable. How will we get there? We may feel so tired, so overwhelmed by all we have learned and endured, that our instincts fail us. Where do we begin? Can there possibly be anyone out there with whom we could trust our precious child, given that we can barely believe we're competent to care for him ourselves?

New parents should begin by clarifying their needs: Do they want an occasional sitter, someone willing to work flexible hours, or a person to come every day? Do they need help doing errands, or someone who can cook a meal, so when both parents return at the end of the day, they can eat something other than whatever was left on the kitchen counter eight hours before? Many parents say they're looking for a caregiver who will do more than sit and read a magazine while their infant naps. Laundry, and trips to the drugstore or dry cleaner, are all chores that somebody has to do. (Once upon a time, that somebody was *you*.) Depleting your bank account to hire a second set of hands can pay huge dividends by relieving you of the "dirty" work so you can spend relaxed, focused time with your child. Make sure the person you hire isn't just doing the "good" stuff—cuddling and reading to your child—leaving you to mop the floor and take out the trash.

Most cities have nanny referral services, if you don't have a willing parent or a child-care center at your place of work. Always ask for a copy of each candidate's birth certificate, as well as a driver's license. Then the hard part begins, meaning you'll have to screen applicants, and talk with them about their past experience. You might try asking candidates about a previous employer, saying something like "Tell me a bit about the last family you worked with. What did you enjoy most about their kids? What was the hardest part of that job?" Then you should call their references, and keep those people on the phone until they're willing to admit something they *didn't* like about their former nanny. Only then will you know if they're telling the whole truth, and if whatever they struggled with will or won't pose a problem for you.

As a last step, you should do a felony check, and also ask to see your potential nanny's health record. But, in the end, you'll have to rely on your instincts. If the person seems calm, energetic, and disciplined, invite her to meet your child. Observe her for an hour or so with your baby. Does she get down to your child's level? Does she speak in a respectful tone of voice? Meeting a new child is a bit like meeting a wild animal. One should approach with alertness and respect for the unpredictability of the response. People who are overeager, or just plain insensitive, may want to touch your child before he's ready. Watch your child for cues. He'll help you know who's right for him.

Let a potential nanny spend her first day watching you with your baby, as you involve him in caregiving activities, like changing a diaper or having a bath. Sometimes a nanny feels she has to look "busy" and so will shake toys in the baby's face—or, worse, jiggle him on her hip while making a meal. You should let her know what your priorities are, and what questions you'll want answers to when you return. What time did the baby fall asleep, for example, or how well did he eat? Sometimes a nanny can find your debriefing sessions intimidating. She may not share your fixation with the regularity of naps or the number of poops. Time, particularly, is a construct that varies from one culture to the next. When you ask your nanny if it took your infant "a long time" to fall asleep, she may not know what you mean.

Spend your nanny's first day close to home, running errands . . . and coming back unannounced. Weigh your disappointment that the kitchen floor is *still* a mess (as it was when you left) against your pleasure at seeing your child happy in the arms of someone else. If you're lucky, you'll hire someone who has skills (or patience) even beyond your own. But try not to drive yourself crazy finding a person to stand in for you (what the courts call *in loco parentis*). Remember, your nanny doesn't have to be perfect. You're not cloning her DNA. And you may have to go through the hiring process again, if the person who's right for you and your newborn ceases to be available or is inappropriate for an older child. You may need to rethink your priorities once your child loves being read to more than rolling around on the ground or building towers with blocks.

Your nanny may give your child funny hairdos, or tell you she's fed your baby "jam" when she means "yam." Try to overlook little divergences in style, especially if they're a product of cultural or generational gaps. If your baby spends only a few hours a week with a baby-sitter, you may choose to let some things slide. The hardest people to monitor are, of course, those who are willing to work for free: a friend, a neighbor, or a member of the family. Grandparents, in particular, consider it their prerogative to spoil a grandchild, and they don't care what *your* rules are; they'll make their own. But you can always tell them that you don't want the television on, or that it's not your policy to spank your child or ply him with sweets. Also, as your child grows, you can explain to him that different people do things differently. The lesson will serve him well as he ventures into the world and meets people from other places (and tries their food).

With caregivers, as with children, boundaries are essential. Your nanny works for you. She isn't your best friend. But don't hesitate to apologize if you make a mistake, the way you would to your child. Try never to correct her—or, heaven forbid, your mother-in-law—in front of your child. You'll want to show your nanny the care she merits as the person in whom you have placed the greatest trust: the trust to love your child when you're not at home. Tell her the truth—don't say you'll be back in an hour if you know you'll be gone all morning. Most important, be honest with your child. Tell even the smallest infant when you plan to leave the house. Don't assume he won't mind if you "sneak away." If you won't be home when he wakes, try saying, "When you get up in the morning, Aurora will put your clothes on and give you breakfast." The less troubled or "guilty" you seem about leaving, the less fretful your baby will be.

Secretly many parents fear, not that their child wilts when they leave, but that he may not be missing them *enough*. Your toddler may even slip and call the nanny "Mommy." Mommies describe this as a dagger to the heart. But believe that your child will always know who you are and be grateful to see you. You are irreplaceable; the nanny is not. If your child tells you he's mad at you for being away, try to acknowledge his feelings. You might say, "It's hard for you that I'm not here in the mornings. But we'll be together all afternoon." The more your child learns to be loved by other people, the safer he'll feel in the world, and the readier he'll be for a playgroup or preschool. By finding a caregiver, you begin to create the village every parent needs to raise a child. That—and a stack of take-out menus—will help you regain control of your schedule and reclaim your peace of mind.

if it ain't broke, don't fix it

baby gear

Car seats and carriers that double as easy chairs, bouncy seats, battery-operated swings, jumpers, walkers, stationary walkers known as "excersaucers"—these are just some of the contraptions in which we park our babies. We tell ourselves, "If I could just get him to sleep, or at least keep him busy, I could get something done."

When we're not putting our babies in devices they can't get out of on their own, we're placing them in postures they can't get *into* on their own, like sitting. How many times have you seen a small baby propped up with pillows, looking like a cross between an elderly convalescent and a sand castle at high tide? "But he gets bored lying on his back," a new father may complain. Did the baby whisper in his ear, "Please, Dad, I need a new perspective on life"? Is it the baby who is bored or the parent?

Most of the books new parents consult say that babies learn to "sit up," or are able to sit unsupported, between six and seven months. What they mean is that your six month old, if deposited on his bottom, can keep himself erect for thirty seconds or so before you have to yell "Timber!" Children who are regularly placed in the "locked and upright position," before they can attain it on their own, sometimes get hurt when they topple over and feel frustrated when they can't resurrect themselves. Few babies can go from lying down to sitting up *on their own* until they begin to crawl. Until then, a baby needs a lap and arms to support him while sitting. In short, he needs the contours of a "human chair."

Your three month old's neck has about as much strength as a strand of linguine. If you're putting him down on his tummy, he may very well need a "new perspective," one that encompasses more than the weave of the rug beneath. When not being held or carried, young babies are most comfortable lying on their backs. This position affords them the greatest mobility, not to mention a better view. Once your child has learned to roll over—you may want to teach your dog this, but not your baby—he'll be game to spend some "quality time" on his belly.

Many of us complain of backache after a long trip in

an airplane seat. But none of us knows the long-term effect on infants of sitting for hours each day in molded plastic car seats or carriers. Only use a car seat when it's absolutely necessary: when your baby's in the car. An eight month old spending as little as twenty minutes a day in stationary walkers may suffer long-term consequences. Physical therapists are seeing more and more children with sway backs and pronated or flat feet. Many of these children will grow up to develop knee, hip, and back problems. While "safer" than jumpers or walkers, which have been linked to numerous accidents, excersaucers force children who can't stand on their own yet to do just that. Such devices are *vises* that limit a child's range of movement and activity— for the convenience of the caregiver. Parents console themselves by saying, "He looks so happy in it," or "It's strengthening his legs for walking," but learning to walk means learning to balance on one foot. Nothing you buy in a store can teach this. Children who spend time in walkers, excersaucers, and jumpers don't walk any earlier or any better than other children. In fact, some doctors and physical therapists believe these devices actually hinder development.

If you need to answer an E-mail or take out the garbage, don't restrain your child, *contain* him. Instead of relying on a swing or stationary walker to keep him "out of trouble," create a safe, enclosed space for him to play. Here he will be free to use his body however he—not some manufacturer—sees fit. What better way for him to learn the limits of his body and develop self-restraint? Besides, a baby who's always strapped in and buckled up, in the absence of danger, is bound to feel hemmed in and help-less. Every time a propped-up baby falls, he must wait for someone to help.

Your baby comes with no assembly required—at least not by you. He will become fully operational when he's good and ready. If you tinker with his automatic timer, you might just throw things out of whack. Your baby spent nine months developing in the womb without the benefit of gear approved by the Juvenile Products Manufacturers Association. Trust the body's wisdom. Your child will be rewarded with self-confidence and grace—the best protec-tion against broken bones and a bruised ego—if you do.

mind over
manners

One kiss, if you're in Mexico. Two kisses, if you're French. Four kisses, two on each cheek, if you're in Lebanon. That's just for starters, when we say "hello." But no greeting is more arcane than that which passes between two toddlers, who may begin their acquaintance by lifting up their shirts. Before you know it, they're examining each other's belly buttons. Is that any more outlandish than what grown-ups do?

Manners are about as complicated as the mating dance between two praying mantises. For young children, such rituals can be especially confusing; as ever, they look to parents to lead the way. But often, grown-ups themselves are nervous or self-conscious. They forget that children perceive social situations differently and often employ their own inscrutable set of rituals. Notice that very young children rarely "perform" their delight at seeing each other. Their faces aren't masks of joy, the way ours can be. Children often wait to see what's going to happen, and this genuine act of seeing underlies all etiquette. In fact, the word *respect* means to "see again," to "reconsider." Children, astute observers that they are, should be naturals at it.

Yet too often children are asked to behave in ways that feel anything but natural; to them, manners can seem abstract or, worse, inauthentic, even insincere. "Say thank you," we instruct our toddler, even before she's holding the juice box her host has offered. The child fails to see the connection between what's given and what her response should be. Better to tell her, "Aunt Carol has handed you a juice box. I'm going to thank her for giving you something to drink." Your child will take note both of the hospitality and your response to it. In most cases, Aunt Carol won't be standing there waiting for an engraved note of thanks, nor will she yank the bottle from your child's hand if none arrives. Think of how glad she will be when a "thank you" comes, of its own accord, in all its spontaneity. No rote response packs nearly the same punch.

The world—which is to say, the playground—will be full of object lessons in errant behavior. Often your child may seem to seek them out. She may be inexorably drawn to the classmate whose parents are his indentured servants, or who seems to have his playmates under his four-year-old thumb. If your child screams, "Get my sandals!" at the top of her lungs, insisting, "That's what Alex does!" remind her, "In Alex's family, it may be all right to make demands like that, but that's not what we do." Such transgressions offer an ideal opportunity to reaffirm the values of your family, and to let your child help define the world in which she lives. Besides, you're trying to nurture a child you'll want to spend time with, one whom you will genuinely enjoy.

But you, too, must be certain never to behave like a banshee, even when you get a parking ticket or lose your keys. Always let your child know if you did something you wish you hadn't, especially if the transgression involves her. Don't be afraid to apologize to her when you lose your temper. Speak kindly of other people, even when they rub you the wrong way. Respect—"seeing again"—means considering your behavior through your child's eyes. Make sure you're someone she can emulate.

Most parents know that good manners begin at home, never stopping to consider whether that home is in Pasadena or Paraguay. What makes appropriate behavior so challenging is that the rules aren't fixed; sensitivity to other people requires flexibility as well as finesse. A parent's job is to help a child learn to take the measure of a situation and to regard others' needs as equal to her own. Manners aren't a suit of armor you clamp onto your child as she leaves your door. They are a compass, a moral compass, to help her navigate the world.

But behaving well requires real feeling, as well as thought. "Good" behavior should make us *feel* good, because it means we're at ease, joyful, reveling in others' company. That's why you don't want to become the "polite police," nagging or bullying your child: You will hate yourself and fill your child with dread. Instead, offer her two reasonable options anytime you think she may feel awkward: "When we get to Joan's house, I'm going to shake her hand. You may do the same, or look her in the eye and say, 'Hello.'" Always give her choices you can live with. Don't ask, "Would you like to say 'Hello,'" unless you're happy to have your child decline and stand frozen, without a word. Very often a child's "shyness" is a product of being put on the spot. You may even appeal to the anthropologist in your child by talking about the relativity of manners. Tell her, "In Arabic, there are many kinds of greetings. You might welcome the day by calling it, 'The Morning of Jasmine,' and your friend might respond by calling it, 'The Morning of Heavy Cream.'" Your child, insatiable researcher that she is, will love being in on the secret, especially if you encourage her to embellish and improvise.

Even so, your child will reserve the right to behave according to her own rules, just as she may greet your guests in a feathered boa and pull-up pants. Treat her as you would any foreign dignitary, with respect for the difference in customs. But always allow for those moments when she may withdraw or seem overwhelmed. Don't feel you need to apologize for her behavior. Just observe, and narrate: "Look, Hannah is wearing her pink boa." You, too, may find yourself seeing anew.

Who knows, next time you offer your cheek—or show someone your belly button—you may imbue the ritual with fresh energy. Like your child, you may welcome a chance to show the world who you really are, especially when greeted by genuine feeling—or the scent of heavy cream—in return.

it's my party
and i'll cry if
i want to

temper tantrums

Is "It's My Party and I'll Cry if I Want To"
the title of a 1963 hit song or the first article in
the Toddler Bill of Rights? When your two-year-old
daughter begins to bawl at her birthday party, your first
thought may be, "How could she, after all the trouble I've
gone to!" "How can I get her to stop?" is likely to be a
close second. Babies cry because they have no other way
of telling you they're hungry, sleepy, or want to be held.
When toddlers and older children cry, they're hurt or frustrated. They need a release no words can provide.

It can be hard for parents living on a time budget to
be sympathetic to the stresses of children. Often it seems

as if the smallest infraction—a pant leg an inch shy of the ankle—is capable of triggering a tantrum. In fact, tantrums are usually the result of an accumulation of "wrongs": being slighted by a friend at preschool, insufficient sleep, the teasing of an older sibling, or the rushing that results from too many scheduled activities. Tantrums happen in public at "the worst possible moment," but they also occur, oddly enough, when you are at home, relaxed, and at your most attentive. What both situations have in common is you: your presence. When your mother, casting a disparaging eye on you and your unhinged child, mutters beneath her breath, "She never behaves this way with me," remind yourself that children reserve this behavior for the people they love most. Instead of wishing your three year old felt a little *less* at ease, try thinking of each tantrum as a trophy: You've won it because your child knows you can go the distance. She isn't trying to manipulate you or ruin a lovely day. She simply can't contain herself any longer and feels safe enough to rage because you're there . . . whether you want to be or not.

You wouldn't dream of asking your child not to sweat or exhale, but how many times have you heard a parent say to a child, "Don't cry"? No parent wants to dampen her child's spirits, but nearly all of us feel compelled to stem our children's tears, telling them they're okay when they're clearly not. We so badly *want* everything to be okay. Remind yourself that crying, which reduces blood pressure, pulse rate, and body temperature, is one way the body eliminates tension. Chronically elevated levels of stress hormones inhibit learning and are even associated with a lower IQ. We should *welcome* tears because they relieve us of these hormones—a waste product of living— much the way a sigh releases excess carbon dioxide. Stressed-out adults have been known to prescribe themselves a hot bath, but for a child there's nothing like a good cry to restore her good humor, her ability to think clearly and act respectfully.

Children do more crying because they live more fully and are less practiced at "holding it in." A child who's graduated from diapers understands she can no longer pee whenever and wherever she wishes. She lets you know she needs "to go," and you react accordingly by looking for the nearest bathroom.

It's usually best to respond similarly to a brewing tantrum. Describe to your child what you see happening ("It looks like you're upset about a lot of things and feel like crying") and tell her the amount of time needed before you can devote yourself fully to her. If necessary, organize your exit to a more appropriate place. When she finally does explode, she may have a litany of complaints, fixate on a specific grievance, or be crying so hard you can't make out her words. Don't try. Your role isn't to defend yourself (that sweater is in the wash), to fix the problem (we'll get another balloon), or to talk her down or out of her fury. Your role is to stay close to her—even hold her—and to listen to and support the way she feels.

Most parents worry that acknowledging a child's painful emotions will prolong the crying. In fact, denying the feelings, by saying, "It's nothing," or, "You're crying over *that?*" is far more upsetting to the aggrieved child. Acknowledging feelings can sound like you're "rubbing it in," but go ahead, rub it in. If your child is crying because Daddy is away, don't say "but he'll be back tomorrow." Try saying, "You *really* miss him, don't you?" or, "You wish he could be here with you *right now.*" The only hard-and-fast rule governing temper tantrums is that your child should not injure herself or you: "I'm not going to let you hit me because it hurts, but here's a pillow you can punch."

Haven't *you* ever felt like clobbering a cushion? For adults, a primary source of stress is powerlessness. Children have very little control over their lives, so it's no wonder they lose control of themselves. It may be *her* party, but Mom and Dad call most of the shots. When your birthday girl begins to sob uncontrollably because her slice of cake doesn't have a candy rose, your first impulse may be to scour the party for a kid whose slice does, and negotiate a swap. Instead, with kind words and loving arms, let your daughter know she can cry if she wants to. That's the best birthday present you can give.

ashes, ashes

There's a Latin proverb, *Veritas odium parfit* (truth begets hatred). But for children, truth begets trust. Children need to believe that you are as good as your word: You *will* return from the supermarket as promised, you *will* read them one more story before bed. If you're constantly backtracking ("I said I'd be here for dinner, but now I won't be home until you're asleep"), children come to feel that nothing is certain. But is there such a thing as too much truth? If the family dog dies, you may not need to share all the details, especially if your child is young. The important thing is to acknowledge his grief, and yours. Young children have an automatic shut-off valve: They are highly self-protective and absorb only as much information as they can understand.

But that doesn't mean that, as a parent, you are off the hook. Weeks later, your child may ask, "Where's Spot?"

Don't say anything that feels false or that you will have to revise or disown later. Most of all, assure him that it's all right to feel sad. Children need to know that all emotions are permissible, but all behaviors resulting from those emotions are not. A child who learns to cry when he's young is probably less likely to end up bawling his eyes out on a therapist's couch.

One of the most important gifts you can give your child is the knowledge that life isn't perfect, and that *you* can't make it perfect. That isn't your job. Steer clear of the narcissistic impulse to "fix" things or to sanitize his world to make your own more habitable. Parents who can't tolerate their children's disappointment rob them of a fundamental right: the right to be unhappy and to learn from loss.

One way to prepare your children is to read to them, even stories that are grim. Such stories allow children to play out unconscious fears or to find a safe outlet for their "wicked" desires. If you rid your child's world of monsters, he may be losing the buddies he identifies with most or the creatures from whom he has most to learn.

Again, take your cues from your child. He'll tell you what his questions are. Information, like medicine, should be given in doses, but resist the impulse to sugar-coat things. It's not always wise to eliminate references to death, the way some teachers at a Jewish preschool did, changing the verse "ashes, ashes" in a favorite nursery rhyme to "one and two and." Many of the toddlers singing "Ring around the rosy" were the grandchildren of Holocaust survivors. Rising from the ashes was their legacy. The bubonic plague, when "Ring around the rosy" came into being, is echoed in other plagues, and future generations will know suffering as well. The sooner our children learn that life is tinged with darkness, the readier they will be to light a light.

seen and not heard

"Oh, look at you! You really want to go for a walk. Tell you what, let me open the mail first and then we'll go out." No, this isn't a sympathetic new father cooing at his infant, it's the master of the house talking to his pooch. Strange as it may seem, many people communicate better with their dogs than with their babies. Your four month old can't bring you a leash, but he *is* trying to tell you something. Are you really listening? While few parents openly subscribe to the belief that children should be "seen and not heard," many of us reflexively insert a pacifier, breast, or bottle into a baby's mouth the minute it opens wide. Flannery O'Connor once said that anyone who's survived infancy has enough stories to last a lifetime. What story is your child telling you?

Nowadays we all pay lip service to the idea that children have a point of view and are entitled to express it. We talk a lot about listening, but what we're really good at is talking and waiting to talk. When our children are babies, we find we need to listen with our eyes as well as our ears, much the way we do with pets, to heed physical cues and facial expressions. "You look like you're having a poo," you might say to your infant, when you note a familiar grimace on his face, or, "You're starting to fidget; I think it's time for your bottle." Notice the look of pleasure on your infant's face when he feels you have really understood.

Once our kids are old enough to tell their stories—the funny thing Ethan did at preschool or the byzantine rules of a game your son's just made up—we may feign attention. "Uh-huh. Uh-huh. Huh," we mutter, while wondering whether the letter we're writing should be signed "Sincerely" or just "Best Regards." In fact, "uh-huh" and "huh" (along with "oh" and "umm") can be great listening words—but only if uttered with utter presence of mind. These words can function like a blank canvas. What better gift to offer your child when he approaches with a brush and palette, wanting to depict his day?

But if you're saying "uh-huh" because you're distracted, level with your child. Tell him, "I want to listen to what you're saying. The problem is I need to concentrate on making dinner. Once I get the roast in the oven, I'm all yours." Most things can wait, but if your child has a burning desire to share something with you, it's probably better for both of you (and for that roast) if you don't keep putting him off.

You'll find that *really* listening isn't so difficult, partly because it doesn't require the constant barrage of questions we tend to bombard our friends with over lunch or on the telephone. Really hearing someone means allowing that person to speak without interruption. People want to be heard, not convinced of *your* point of view. Many of us have come home upset by a disagreement with our boss, wanting nothing so much as to "vent," only to have our spouse cut short the conversation with what seems an "easy solution." When someone *listens* to us, as opposed to giving us unsolicited opinions or answers, we're able to get a handle on our emotions. Then, if need be, we can forge a plan of our own for dealing with the problem. Sometimes just being heard is solace enough.

When children broach a subject, parents tend to say too much or ask too many questions, thereby dominating or derailing the conversation. Questions can be like speed bumps—or worse still, detours on the route to meaningful exchange. Your child may decide to ditch the topic and turn his attention to his Legos or, later, to his on-line friends. Besides, direct questions like, "Why did you do that?" rarely produce satisfying answers. You'll have better luck if you voice an observation or hazard a guess, as in, "You really didn't like what Nora said to you." When asking questions, make them as specific as possible. Instead of, "How was preschool today?" try, "Who did you play with after nap time?" Chances are your child will abandon his dry, executive summary for a vivid account of his day, if he knows you are really tuned in to its particulars.

Healthy communication with your child begins at the beginning. Talk to your newborn about what you're doing whenever you bathe him, feed him, change his diaper, or comb his hair. When he begins to talk back—and he will, delightedly—try not to correct him. If he points and says "ba," you don't need to grab the object, hold it in front of his face, and loudly enunciate B . . . A . . . L . . . L, as if he were a foreign emissary whose translator had nodded off. If you've ever studied another language, you know how useless it is to be drilled in isolated vocabulary words. The good language instructor was the one who said, "Use *parapluie* in a sentence," not "*Parapluie*—umbrella. Repeat after me." *You* may be struggling to understand your toddler, but don't assume *he*'s struggling with a word. He thinks he's saying "ball" correctly. Simply nod your head and observe, "You're pointing to the ball."

Likewise, you don't need to correct your toddler's grammar. If he exclaims, "I winned," you'll only confuse him and curtail his enthusiasm by replying, "I *won*." Better to respond by saying, "You won? That's great!" Model the proper usage, and it will begin to seep into his conversation effortlessly.

The real modeling begins with an older child, one who won't put his toys away or sit properly in a chair. Nagging him never gets you anywhere, any more than it produced anything but resentment in us when *we* were nagged. And he'll appreciate being accused of things about as much as your spouse does. Wagging your finger may work for your dog, but not for your child. It's far wiser, and more effective, to approach matters indirectly, saying something like, "The faucet needs to be turned off; I hate to see water wasted," rather than, "You're always leaving the water running. I've told you time and time again. . . ." Your request comes through more vividly without the accusation. Another tactic for getting children to listen is to use fewer words. The word "faucet!"—whether you shout, sing, or whisper it—will compel your child to think. If he has to supply the missing words (this is great practice for all those standardized tests he'll soon be taking), he'll be more likely to remember in the future. The faucet will get turned off, and your anger, too, will have been staunched.

The next time your child leaves the faucet running

(and it will happen again), don't despair. As the writer James Baldwin said, "Children have never been very good at listening to their elders, but they have never failed to imitate them." If our children don't seem to listen to anything we say, it's because *we* pay so little attention. We need to show our children what it means to really listen, just as we need to edit the way we speak to them, so that they, in turn, will listen to us. It is said that we speak what we already know, but learn by listening . . . even if it's to a story about the Power Puff Girls. If you learn to hold your tongue from time to time, you'll find that your child is more than willing to lend *you* his ears. If you don't, it may be you who is seen but not heard.

mirror, mirror
on the wall

seeing, not judging

Your child doesn't want to be told she's the fairest. She wants to know, "Do I have freckles, is my hair curly, is my skin the color of apricots or coffee beans?"

What we all crave is to be seen, *really* seen, and through that seeing, know ourselves. We spend much of our life—in work, love, friendship, and sometimes even in therapy—trying to achieve this.

"Mommy, Mommy," your child cries, toes curled over the edge of the diving board. "Look at me!" The parent's role is to look and, when called upon, to describe what he or she sees: "You're on the diving board!" The see-er is not, and should not aspire to be, a seer: "You're going to be a champion diver someday!" Think sportscasting, not forecasting. It is not your point of view the child is longing for, but simply that you *view*.

When your attention has not been requested, unsolicited comments may be just that. "Look at you, way up there on the high dive!" to a child deep in concentration may induce fear or put pressure on her to perform.

Parents should set limits for their children but avoid limiting them as people by judging or labeling them: "He's a good eater," or "She's an easy baby." Sometimes we use labels to mold children into the people we want them to become. As a child grows, the label applied to her becomes something she feels she can't live up to or may want to live down.

Even praise can constrain. It can divert a child from soaring on the wings of her true interests and desires, keeping her to the safe tarmac of that which has proven praiseworthy. When you wish to laud your child, be descriptive and specific. "Wow! You made your friend feel so welcome when you served her that glass of milk. And you poured it all by yourself." What busy parent with divided attention hasn't said "beautiful painting" or "good girl"? Think twice about remarks that describe the forest on the basis of one tree or are so generic they could apply to anyone. Such comments are silver shiny but also slippery. Their effect disappears quicker than a sardine down a circus seal's throat.

Help your child see her true self, and to her own self she'll be true.

the committee
of sleep

getting your baby to bed

John Steinbeck once said, "It is a common experience that a problem difficult at night is resolved in the morning after the committee of sleep has worked it out." Yet sleep itself is frequently the biggest problem for new parents: Researchers have discovered that sleep is as great a national obsession for Americans as eating is for Italian parents.

Babies in the United States, however, sleep less on average than children in many other countries. (Dutch children, for example, sleep at least two hours more per night.) In our haste to make our lives more "efficient," we have downsized sleep, not just for children, but for ourselves. While we despair over our loss of sleep and its effect on our productivity, we introduce an ever-greater number of obstacles, including home offices, cable channels, and chat rooms.

The committee of sleep provides little comfort because the "experts" do not speak with one voice. They recommend sleeping with your baby . . . and never sleeping with your baby. Responding to his cries at timed intervals . . . or not at all. Some parents put their wakeful babies in the car and drive them around to get them to fall asleep. Others put a restive infant in a car seat on top of the dryer. Meanwhile, some evolutionary biologists believe that newborns, with their immature nervous systems, are not meant to sleep too deeply after all. Not only have we learned to put babies down on their backs—to reduce the incidence of Sudden Infant Death Syndrome (SIDS)—but we've even been advised to turn baby monitors the wrong way around. That way our infants can hear us as we breathe, stir, and mumble dreamily. And at least *someone* would be getting some rest.

Many parents, of course, opt to dispense with technology altogether and let the baby sleep in their room, even in their own bed. If you or your partner is a light sleeper, sharing quarters with your baby could make for miserable bedfellows. But if you're a parent who needs to stick your finger under your baby's nose every time you wake to make sure he's still breathing, you're probably going to want to keep him close. After all, he was in the womb for nine months. Just because he's "out" doesn't mean you have to exile him. Your mother-in-law may warn that "you'll never get him out of your bed" once you let him sleep there, but you will, if you really put your mind to it.

But how? First, you have to be willing to give up your fear that your baby is cold, hungry, or incapable of drawing a breath without you hovering nearby. Rest assured: It's never too late to introduce your child to new sleeping accommodations or to devise a new routine. If your ten month old is accustomed to sleeping next to you or in your bed, it may take him awhile to adjust to a crib in his own room, but he *will* adjust. If you had done it sooner, *you* might have had trouble adjusting, since some parents can't get back to sleep once they've made the long march into their child's room for a feeding at 3 A.M.

Fortunately, what's best *in the long run* is the same for babies and their parents: sleep, downy sleep. When you're ready for your child to learn to fall asleep—or fall back asleep—on his own, you'll find it easier if he's in his own crib in another room. Don't kid yourself: You *will* have to listen to some crying, which is your baby's only means of communicating with you. If you turn a deaf ear, or use earplugs, you send your baby the message that you know he's unhappy and you don't care. Learn to read his cries the way an ornithologist understands birdcalls, to determine if he's thirsty, sick, or just too tired to drop off.

Some babies need to discharge excess energy before they can surrender to sleep. Tell your baby that you hear him crying, and that it's okay to cry. Every baby is different, and the edicts of the committee of sleep tend to be rigid and punitive. It's not that you should *never* hold your baby or rock him to sleep, it's that you should save these more drastic measures for the nights when basic first aid—simply patting him, then walking out of the room—won't help.

One thing most sleep advisors agree on is that your baby should love his crib and spend time there from his earliest days. Putting him to sleep in the crib while he's still awake is always preferable. Otherwise, if he has dozed off in your arms or at your breast, he may be startled and even afraid if he wakes up "behind bars." How quickly he falls asleep in his crib is largely dependent on whether or not you've established a bedtime routine. Sleep routines are a little like a play rehearsal. Your baby hears his "cue," which could be a simple story or lullaby after lights are out, and then performs his part.

Every baby comes with his own prewired settings, but you may find that you need to adjust his "default" mode. If you want to customize your baby's sleep rhythms because he's not getting enough sleep—or because his sleep patterns are disruptive to everyone else—your best bet is to institute regular nap and bedtimes. You *will* be making a trade-off, as is the case with any parenting decision: You forfeit flexibility, and even adaptability, for predictability. But if you know your baby will nap for two hours every afternoon, you can finish that budget report or call the plumber—and even get some shut-eye yourself! If you need to travel with your baby or can't afford a baby-sitter, you'll probably want a baby who can fall asleep on-the-go, and who can vary his hours somewhat. The baby accustomed to a single routine and one set of sleep accommodations isn't likely to snooze in his stroller or on a lambskin rug at a Mozart festival.

But beware of varying your routine too much and of pushing back bedtime to accommodate your late day. In the Netherlands, parents worship at the altar of routine (one reason their children may sleep better). They also believe in putting them to bed *early*. If you're working late, and are desperate to spend some time with your little one, try scheduling your playtime *before* work. If you get up an hour or so earlier, you won't have to race out of the house without breakfast . . . and you'll get to spend unhurried, undistracted time with your baby, when he's fresh and at his best.

Overtired babies and toddlers have a tough time settling down to rest. This is one of the many paradoxes of sleep: the more it's needed, the more elusive it seems. Your baby—or rather, your human alarm clock—may wake you regularly at 4:00 A.M., but putting him to sleep later won't help you sleep in. If you want your baby to snooze until, say, 6:00 A.M., try putting him to bed an hour or two *earlier*. The Bible is one book we wouldn't dream of consulting to solve our sleep problems, but perhaps we should, because *sleep begets sleep*. A late nap may delay bedtime, but a long one, properly timed, is more like an appetizer before the main dish. And remember: You may have to readdress your child's sleep routine once he's learned to walk or started preschool. Developmental leaps tend to wreak havoc with the status quo, and your baby's sleep patterns are often and easily disrupted by change.

You'll never again sleep like a baby once you've had one, but there's nothing more beautiful, even to exhausted eyes, than the sight of your infant asleep. A beatific smile, as inscrutable as Buddha's, flits across his face, and you can't help but wonder what he's dreaming of. Don't spend too much time thinking about it. Try to avert your adoring gaze and get some rest.

take my wife, please!

s h a r i n g

Have you ever wished you could loan out your husband—the way museums do paintings—and hang a little sign where he used to sit? Most of us, at some point or other, have longed for temporary relief from our spouse. That's why the Henny Youngman line, "Take my wife, please!" gets laughs. But how funny would it be if your mother hissed at you, "Be nice! Let your neighbor Jeanine have a turn . . . with your husband"? There are some things we just don't want to share.

Sharing is serious business, especially for parents who feel mortified every time their toddler won't relinquish a toy. They worry that they're nurturing a narcissist, but they're forgetting: Possession is nine-tenths of the law. Your child must first *possess*—and even be possessive of—

her rubber tyrannosaurus before she can possibly offer it to a friend. Instead of wincing every time your two year old growls, "Mine!" remind yourself that she's doing "prep work," the kind you do before your dinner guests arrive. She's claiming for herself something she needs and deserves to own. Only then will her act of sharing carry any weight.

If you want to ensure a smooth and relatively speedy transition from "Mine!" to "You can try my tricycle if you want," set a good example. Be giving yourself and giving *of* yourself. It's easy, of course, to lend or give away what we don't particularly like (many a toddler has offered to "share" broccoli with her baby brother), but if you want your child to be truly generous, share with her the things she knows *you* love. If you let your three year old wear your string of pearls ("only in this room and please don't pull on it"), she learns not just about sharing, but also about trust, and the responsibility that comes with it.

You also want to help your child feel comfortable, comfortable enough to be generous. If your three year old wants to bring a bucket and shovel to the park, let her know, *before* leaving the house, that other children may want to play with them. If she's not keen on that idea, suggest leaving the toys at home. Similarly, when a friend is coming for a play date, ask your child, *before* the friend arrives, if there are any toys "too special" to share. Assist your child in putting these toys away. And when *your* child is the one invited, you might even suggest to the host parent that she banish anything her little one can't live without or doesn't want to share.

A good guest never shows up empty-handed. Neither should your three year old. While she needn't bring a bouquet or bottle of Beaujolais, she might want to bring a backpack with some of her own toys (to take home again when she leaves). If her host isn't behaving hospitably, your child will at least have some toys to enjoy. More likely than not, the child you are visiting will appreciate the gesture (or become so engrossed in your child's stash) that he will reciprocate with his version of *mi casa es tu casa:* He'll open his own toy chest.

There is no way to eliminate conflict during a play date, nor should you wish to, because conflict is one of your child's greatest teachers. When playmates under the age of two covet the same toy, most of the time all you really need to do is "sportscast." "You both want the wheelbarrow. Miriam is pulling on one side, and you're pulling on the other. I'm going to get a little closer to make sure you're both safe." By describing what you see, you give the children perspective on their physical sensations. Your words allow them to grasp the problem, while your watchful presence gives them the security to work things out. With children this age, one of them usually lets go of the wheelbarrow and looks for something else to amuse herself.

With older toddlers and preschoolers (who've graduated from "Mine!" to "Not fair! I had it first"), the problem can get thornier. You'll probably need to modify your sportscasting technique. Instead of simply narrating what you see, you'll also want to describe what the children appear to be feeling in a way that represents them without taking sides. When two children are fighting over a toy, your job is to help *them* resolve the conflict, making sure that no one gets hurt in the process. You want to mediate, not legislate. You may find, however, that you need to take the "bone of contention" away from whoever has it. Doing so evens the playing field and promotes a calmer atmosphere, one more conducive to dialogue. If you don't have time to see the problem through, say, "I'm putting this doll away for now because the baby is crying upstairs. You can try to work it out on your own or wait for me to come back."

It's a natural, even honorable, impulse to defend the child who is smaller, but it's an inappropriate response when two kids are squabbling. It's not that you should make light of their dispute. On the contrary, treat them like heads of state arguing over a common border. As a United Nations interpreter, you'd be out of line telling one party to give back the north bank or escorting the other to an anteroom for a time-out. Time *away* from each other, on the other hand, can help feuding children cool down enough to resume negotiations.

Sharing is among any child's greatest challenges, and kids need our compassion and patience while they learn to part with beloved objects or borrow cherished toys. Remind yourself of that whenever your toddler refuses to let anyone touch her tea set or denies a parched visitor a drink from one of *her* sippy cups. Remember that you, too, have things you won't part with. You'll never want to loan your husband to your neighbor. But your child, given a chance to share at her own pace, may one day surprise you with her graciousness.

thought for food

focusing on food

Imagine your boss and her husband are coming for dinner. You're making your special chicken with Rice Crispy sauce. Your boss's husband politely declines a helping. You would no sooner say, "Just try one bite, please; then you can have a cookie!" than you would volunteer to tuck a napkin into his shirt.

Yet parents regularly cajole children to try new foods or bribe them with dessert to get them to eat. While we offer them many choices—would you like a bath before or after dinner? Do you want to play indoors or out?—we insist that they eat only what the grown-ups are eating, even when it's spicy or strange smelling or . . . squash. Eating is the only arena in which small children can exert their power: They can't vault out of the crib to protest a nap, but they *can* clamp shut their jaw. Even the most respectful parents rarely take no for an answer. "She's a good eater" rivals "He's a Nobel Laureate" as a proud parent's favorite phrase.

We all remember digging into that tub of Cool Whip when we got home from school, and certainly a little saturated fat never hurt anyone. But children today eat more poorly than ever, despite the greater availability of fresh produce and organic foods. Fast-food, jumbo-sized portions and the omnipresence of TV have combined to undermine many families' eating habits. Now that schools have eliminated daily recess—only the state of Virginia still requires it by law—and many kids come home from school to an empty house, the television and a jumbo bag of chips have become their most reliable buddies. Remember the story of "Hansel and Gretel"? Hansel, in a cage being fattened by the old woman, is a cousin to the child allowed to sit all day in the front of the tube, stuffing himself. Only the evil that consumes him isn't an ugly witch, it's the threat of diabetes, cancer, or heart disease for which his eating habits put him at greater risk.

Parents who exorcise their child's television or computer in favor of exercise might consider pulling the plug on their own habit as well. Here's an instance where the apple, especially if it's candied, doesn't fall far from the tree: A child of overweight parents is 80 percent likelier to be fat. Many adults "multitask" even at the dinner table: They read and eat, or watch *Jerry Springer* while snacking, to say nothing of those who drive while wolfing down a Whopper. Only by focusing on your food, lingering over it, will you know how it tastes and when you've had enough. When children eat, we want them to read their body's cues—not the baseball scores—so they can locate and react to their innate shut-off valve.

Children should be discouraged from bringing toys to the table, just as you would ban your phone list or office brief. Likewise, try to avoid coaxing a younger child by playing "choo-choo" with the spoon; otherwise, you'll feel like a hypocrite when you one day chide him for playing with his food. Instead, *involve* him in the meal, letting him control what he eats, even the size of his portions. (Studies show that when kids serve themselves, as opposed to having parents heap food on their plates, they eat more and waste less food.) If you offer him two choices, knowing one (pasta or rice) is a surefire hit, you'll risk less frustration, while guaranteeing that he's consumed something other than the bright blue rocket ship ice cream cake at the birthday party next door. Don't, however, serve potato chips, spinach, and chicken and be surprised when the only sound you hear is *crunch*. Your child may be allowed to choose, but as always, you set the parameters, deciding among which foods he will choose.

Try to be flexible, allowing children to change their minds: Reintroduce a food that wasn't a hit last night in several weeks or months. And don't be a bean counter: People who meticulously calculate how far a full tank of gas takes them, or how much laundry detergent to use per load, must abandon their abacuses when it comes to food. No healthy child allows himself to go hungry. Parents should look at consumption over a matter of days to get a true picture of what their child eats.

But the fact that so many Norman Rockwell paintings feature a family meal tells us something: Eating and conversation at the dinner table are as American as. . . . In fact, few families regularly eat together; when they do, the meal is often more contest—Whose day was crazier? Who'll grab the last ear of corn?—than repast. Yet families should strive to make the shared meal a priority, even creating their own rituals, like inviting each person to recount a favorite moment of the day. Such involvement can begin hours, even days, before the meal, when you take your child to the grocery store or invite him to help measure ingredients into a bowl. (Both are good ways to help a child learn math.) Assign even the smallest participant a task: shelling peas, putting dandelions in a vase on the table. Making your toddler your *sous-chef* will show him that the kitchen is a livelier place than any video screen. You may discover that you, too, enjoy his participation,

to say nothing of the pleasure of seeing him eat. Together you may discover new recipes, like dirt soufflé or
pasta with freshly grated bark. Just don't try serving *that*
to your boss.

days of whine
and roses

w h i n i n g

If for parents a tantrum is like a bug bite—painful but finite—whining is the verbal and emotional equivalent of a hovering mosquito. The pest's infuriating buzz—as difficult to sleep through as a car alarm—fades away, only to return again and again.

You may try to ignore the whining, but doing so rarely provides the desired result, any more than ignoring the pesky mosquito brings you peace. When ignored, your child may simply decide to "turn up the volume." However, it *is* useful to tell him how you feel about the whining. Doing so relieves some of your frustration and teaches your child the value of expressing emotion. Try telling your child, "I find it hard to help you when you whine at me." Or better yet, avoid blaming him by saying, "I feel impatient and annoyed when I hear whining."

We may all wish the world were whine-free, just as we feel we'd be better off without the maddening mosquito. But it's helpful to think of whining as a low-grade fever. Some of us take aspirin at the first sign of a fever—because we feel lousy and because it's available—but the fever isn't the illness; it's the body's mechanism for battling infection. The most expeditious route to recovery may involve letting the fever run its course, provided it doesn't soar too high. An overly accommodating parent, one who fulfills the whiner's every request, acts a little like aspirin: The child, and the parent, too, may experience some temporary relief, but the underlying condition persists. The myriad "mini needs" expressed by a whining child mask his larger need to cry, and his parent may mistakenly believe that, by attending to them all, he or she can nip a tantrum in the bud. There may be occasions when it's necessary to postpone or delay a tantrum, but that's all you're doing. After you've changed your child's blue plastic spoon for a purple one and the purple for a yellow, you may feel like you're using that very spoon to bail a sinking ship.

Remember the illness metaphor: Often a fever needs to climb before it can break. After you've told your child four times why he can't see his best friend *now*, turned his room upside down looking for his stuffed zebra, and kept his peas from inappropriate intimacy with his fish sticks, it's time to put your foot down, for your child's sake . . . and yours. In a firm but calm voice, decline to meet his next demand. "You want me to get your bear pajamas, but we've just finished putting on the striped ones. I don't want to change pajamas. Tonight you've been needing a lot of attention, but nothing I do helps for very long. It's hard when I don't do what you want, but I can hold you if you feel like crying. Maybe that will help." Once your child is able to unleash his tears, the fever will break and you can look forward to spending time with a calm, agreeable child—in short, a *well* child.

So whether you decide not to change the purple plastic spoon for a yellow one, or to keep the bear pajamas tucked in their drawer, rest assured that you're not being a cold-hearted parent. When you've reached *your* limit, set a limit, and remember: Your child's confinement to his striped pajamas can be the key to your liberation . . . and his.

potty on!

learning to use the toilet

The toilet is almost as much of a taboo in American culture as the humor that's said to emanate from it. When new homeowners "upgrade," one of the first areas they tackle is the toilet, spending untold sums on the gleaming paper dispenser and the low-flush john. But we all dread the "toilet learning" of our toddler because we can't figure out how to make it simple and hygenic . . . and get it over with quickly. About the only thing we dislike more than dirty diapers is the process by which children graduate from them, leaving us swabbing puddles even as we mop our brow.

Part of the problem is that despite all the attention devoted to the subject, no one quite knows how, or when, the ideal transition takes place. When *we* were little, children were "trained" to use the toilet, just as they were bottle-fed on schedule rather than on demand. (Forty years ago, 92 percent of eighteen month olds were toilet trained; now only 2 percent of toddlers are diaper-free by the time they're two.) Like any developmental shift, it's best if the idea comes from your toddler. He may be inspired by his experiences in a playgroup or preschool. Most preschools accept children who are still in diapers; any school that insists you force your child onto the potty before he's ready isn't a place that will make other developmental adjustments with grace and sensitivity.

But how do you know if your toddler is ready? One indication may be his love affair with the word "No." Your child may insist on spearing his own pasta, or snapping the snaps on his sweater. He's ready to do things for himself, rather than relying on you. He may also be following you into the bathroom and sitting there with you while you . . . sit there. Two year olds love a good conversation, and there's no better place to corner you with questions about what happens when the sun burns out or what to name his truck. Help him focus on what you're doing, and let him watch as you wipe yourself, flush the toilet, and wash your hands. You don't want your toddler to think it's a time for playing—wrapping himself, mummylike, in toilet paper—rather than for concentrating on his body's needs.

You'll also know your toddler is ready when he becomes more aware of his dirty diaper and more uncomfortable with it. He may even begin to help you change it, and at the least, he'll have much less tolerance for a "heavy load." You may notice that he likes to go to a private place—a corner of the room or under the table—when defecating. Or you may detect a familiar grimace on his face. Say, "It looks like you're pooping now," or whatever language you and your family have chosen. When you see that telltale expression the next time, encourage him, "It looks like you're about to make a b.m. There's a toilet in the bathroom, if you'd like to use it, like Mommy and Daddy do." Help your child sit on the big toilet, and hold him there; or, better yet, buy him a small, plastic potty. Let your little one accompany you to the store and choose it, and keep it, shiny and welcoming, in the corner of your bathroom. But don't put the new potty in your toddler's bedroom or in the kitchen. Remember, you'll want him to learn to get to the bathroom on time, not anywhere else.

During the day, you might ask your child, "Would you like to use the potty?" but try not to pressure him. You don't want him to feel anxiety about making the transition. Trust that he'll catch on eventually. Everybody does. Similarly, try not to overpraise him when he makes that giant step toward peeing or pooping in the toilet. He may well stand there, looking down into the swirling water, admiring his creation: "Look, Mommy, my poo looks like a dolphin!" Don't laugh, but don't get the camcorder either. Try to take this, and all developmental milestones, in stride.

Some parents insist on giving their child a sticker every time he uses the potty. Any external reinforcement sends the wrong message, that the child is "performing" for someone else's pleasure, not his own. Eating, using the bathroom, resting in the afternoon (your toddler may be giving up his nap around now, too) aren't things your child does to please you. He's doing them to help himself, and to care for his body respectfully. You want him to develop the inner resources, and the inner awareness, to know . . . when he's got to go.

Many people find the bathroom a comforting place to sit and think, and they're grateful for the quiet and privacy. Make sure it has adequate light and heat, and even a basket of kids' magazines near the john in the event of a long wait. Some parents amass a whole library in the bathroom, but it's hard to listen to your body's cues when you're listening to a story, too. Besides, you don't want your child to need company in the bathroom, or he may have trouble using the potty on a play date or at school.

You can also help your toddler become more independent by dressing him in simple clothing, without the worrisome buttons and zippers that would keep even Houdini under wraps. As your child becomes more comfortable, you can spend less time in the bathroom with him; you'll no longer be fixed, like a gargoyle, on the edge of the tub, staring at him as he stares back. Instead, find a chore to do just within earshot. That way you can casually wander in to check on him or to help him wash his hands. But don't panic if he flushes the toilet and immediately jams his fingers back into his mouth. Americans have unreasonable fears about cleanliness. You may need to double up on the paper toilet-seat protectors when you're in a public bathroom, but don't visit your phobias on your little one. He's got enough to contend with just focusing his aim.

The hardest thing for parents, and preschoolers, is the moment when it all goes wrong and your child goes in his pants, or on the rug. Your "big boy" may melt, tears streaming down his face even as a puddle forms beneath his legs. Try to acknowledge his feelings by saying, "You went pee-pee in your underwear. Did you want to get to the bathroom, but couldn't? It's hard when that happens. Maybe next time you'll be able to." You might even discuss strategies with your child so he'll have a plan for the future, like asking a teacher to remind him. Some schools insist that a child wear a diaper for the rest of the day after an "accident." Others allow you to bring a change of clothing and store it in his cubbyhole. In any event, you don't want to embarrass your child or suggest that maybe he's not ready to take this step. Likewise, if he tells you he wants to sleep without a diaper, let him. Just keep a protective pad over the mattress. Let plastics be your friend.

But disposable diapers are perhaps *too* user-friendly, and kids can remain in them for hours—happy, stinky, and unconcerned. With cloth diapers, children were more aware of being wet or dirty. They were perhaps better able to sense what their bodies were doing and to begin to read their body's cues. You might consider letting your child run around the house naked for a few days when he starts to learn about the toilet. That way, his body's signals won't be muffled by a diaper, and he can sense what's happening and respond appropriately. What we want is for our children to become attuned to their own physical sensations, just as we must learn to follow their lead. Your toddler may show no interest in the process, or lose interest, or want to wear diapers beneath his underwear. Or he may hold his waste for periods of time so lengthy it would put even a camel to shame. Just hang in there and keep in mind that the transition to the toilet will liberate you, to say nothing of the money you'll save on diapers and the relief of leaving the two-ton diaper bag at home. This leap in your child's development is cause for (quiet) celebration. So turn on the bathroom light, keep the lid up . . . and potty on!

the color of
water

r e c o g n i t i o n   v e r s u s   p r a i s e

It is said that failure is an orphan and success has many parents. Your child—now a CEO at a Fortune 500 company—may be a chip off the old block, "her father's daughter," but her success wasn't fathered by you. Sometimes we forget that our children's achievements belong to them and claim them for ourselves as a bonus for all our hard work. We strive to ensure our children a safe passage—and harder still, struggle to secure their happiness. When they behave in ways that make *us* happy—kicking the diaper habit, for instance—we cannot contain ourselves and exclaim, "I'm so proud of you!" We may utter this phrase out of love, but it can sound condescending, or as though we're patting ourselves on the back.

"Hurray! Now you're finally able to use the toilet. I've been doing it for years."

One of our jobs as parents is to bear witness to our children's journey. It isn't easy to stand back and watch, to narrate, but when we do we help our children understand who they are and how fully they exist apart from us. When your toddler is struggling to accomplish something, whether it's mustering the dexterity to open a jar or the courage to go down the slide at the park, it's better to describe the situation and acknowledge the look on her face than to say glibly, "You can do it! It's easy." If your toddler's not ready to go down the slide, assurances aimed at calming her fears and boosting her self-confidence may only undermine her. When observing your child, state as simply as you can what she is doing and how she appears to be feeling. "You're trying to take the top off that jar. It's hard. You look like you're getting frustrated," or, "You've climbed all the way to the top and you're seeing how the playground looks from there. Are you thinking about how to go down? You can use the slide or go back down the ladder." Real success has less to do with realizing goals than with feeling good about the decisions you make along the way. And success, as we all know, breeds more of the same.

What we don't know, really, are our children, even

though we think we do. We neglect to observe them closely; in place of genuine insight, we offer them opinions—our opinions. Be generous with your "eye," but stingy with "I." When your child's beaming because she has buckled her sandals all by herself, she needs you to notice and comment on *her* feelings, not your own. Instead of saying, "I'm so proud of you," try observing, "You've put on your shoes yourself!" We parents give and give until our pockets are empty and our hearts ache. The real challenge, however, lies not in giving but in *giving back*—the way a lake gives back the sky its blue.

crime and punishment

discipline

As parents, we want to be "cool," to avoid seeming oppressive or volatile. We don't want to spank our kids or wash out their mouths with soap. As worthy inheritors of the '60s, we believe in nonviolent intervention. We're the generation who, when asked to state our life's goal in a high school yearbook, quoted the writer E. M. Forster: "Only connect."

But discipline *is* about connection, about really seeing your toddler . . . even when you don't like what you see. Children, like adults, may become aggressive because they feel unheard. Don't add insult to injury by trying to ignore them when they misbehave. Your child wants your attention, just as we hanker to be recognized when we berate another driver or belittle a salesperson. The response our children want is for us to show our connection to them, and to demonstrate respect even when we discipline them.

Connect, too, by reacting *swiftly* to a perceived transgression. A delayed response can often confuse a child. But responding immediately doesn't mean shouting or smacking your three year old. For starters, it means taking a deep breath. Try, despite your upset, to think for a moment about what your child has done and why. Only then can you craft an appropriate response. "Reflect, respect, respond" should be your motto. Forget about the rod and the spoiled child.

"Only connect" also describes the proper relationship between your child's misbehavior and your response. The punishment—if that's not too grand a word—must fit the crime. The youngest children benefit only when they see a causal connection: Throwing food results in a speedy departure from the dinner table, not in the cancellation of tomorrow's play date, just as hitting someone with a toy shovel means you'll take the shovel away, not deprive your child of the fairy wand promised days ago. But sometimes parents are too angry or tired to respond. Don't be afraid to tell your child you need some time to think. Otherwise, you risk sputtering out the first, furious words that come to mind, which is why generations of children have been blasted with the cry, "No dessert!"

When two children tussle, separate them, but don't

assume that one child is to blame and should be banished, even if that child is usually the aggressive one. Invite even the smallest child to share her perspective on what happened. Let both children know that their feelings matter to you. (Once, that is, you've taken away the toy in question or separated the feuding four year olds.) Ask, "What were you doing?" not as an exercise in humiliation but in case there's a genuine misunderstanding about your rules. And let children, especially guests, know what kind of behavior is permissible. They can only fulfill the expectations you've announced. As hosts, we constantly signal our adult visitors, gesturing them to the couch, tucking a coaster under their drink. Do the same with your smaller guests, telling them there's no eating in the living room and no bouncing on the Barcalounger. You'll be surprised at how respectful and responsive children are when they feel they've been trusted to be "good."

Most of the time the child you have to discipline is your own, and that's often where the trouble lies. "Only connect" means, too, that we have difficulty shaking the link between the way our parents treated us and the way we treat our child. Adults who were shouted at, humiliated, even hit as children often resort to those practices reflexively. We don't want to, but we may feel we're being "wimps" if we don't. Or we go out of our way *not* to discipline, not wanting to act with the repressive authority we resisted as kids, and find ourselves with children who don't listen or cooperate. Kids don't like to play with kids who are disruptive or bossy, who don't respect rules or respond to the word "No." You do your child a service when you point out antisocial behavior, especially if you do so privately. Take her into another room to talk, but don't insist on a "time out," anymore than you would offer her a sticker for behaving well. Our goal is not to make our children dependent on external reinforcement, but to help them connect to an inner equilibrium and restraint.

Sometimes inviting your child to cool off in a separate room *can* help, by allowing her to think about what's happened without feeling ostracized. Let her choose when she's ready to come out and rejoin society, unless she wants to remain on her own to play. Sometimes smaller children need to be removed forcibly, especially if they've shown an inclination to bite. Tell them biting is never okay and place your hand between them and their putative victim. You might try saying, "If you feel like biting, I'll give you something to chew on, like a plastic toy, but you may not bite another child. If you do, we'll have to go home." Let them know the consequences of even a little kick, shove or nibble, and stick to your guns, despite the discomfort it may cause. Remember that often aggression in the smallest children comes from excitement: the desire to touch, to connect.

In the end, we don't want to deny our kids the freedom to make mistakes or to play in ways that are exuberant, even unrestrained. We don't want to transform them into automatons. That's not what discipline is for. Children thrive when given clear boundaries because they feel safe—safe enough to experiment, to discover who they are. They learn that actions have consequences, both internal and external: a perfect preparation for the teenager your toddler will become (and sometimes already resembles). By helping her to connect, you assist her in "finding herself," another mission our '60s forebearers urged on us. A child who learns both the joy of self-expression and the demands of self-discipline is a child who may wind up in *her* yearbook being voted "most likely to succeed."

sticks and
stones

t e a s i n g

With her ringlets and rosy cheeks, the little girl looked like something out of Norman Rockwell, but her vocabulary sounded more like the Wu-Tang Clan. In the bakery with her mother, the three year old dropped a muffin on the floor. "Damn!" she said. Her mother looked concerned; the other patrons, horrified. The little girl registered their shock. "Well, at least I didn't say 'shit!' "

But children do say "shit" or anything else they've heard their parents say. We parents are always telling our children to "use their words," never imagining they'll use words they picked up from *us*. Don't forget that you have a human sponge in your house, one who absorbs everything. When you drop a glass in the kitchen and say,

"Damn!" your child registers your response. Children quickly deduce that expletives have a lot of power, especially to upset adults. What simpler way to get Mommy to turn on the fireworks? If your child uses an inappropriate word, try to react calmly or with humor, especially if the word is directed at you. When your daughter calls you a "poopoohead," don't drag her into the bathroom to wash out her mouth with soap. "You can call me that if you want," you may begin, "but just don't call me . . . peanut butter breath!" "Peanut butter breath!" she'll shriek, taking to it like a dog to a bone.

Teasing is a natural phase in the life of any preschooler. It's a chance for her to flex her verbal muscle, test the limits of language, and let her imagination fly. You set the parameters, just as you do when you create a safe physical space. Make a safe *verbal* space by letting your child know what is and isn't okay. Similarly, when two children get into a teasing match, make sure they're both enjoying it, letting off steam. Ask each participant, "Is it okay with you to be teased?" If not, tell the other child, "Georgia doesn't want to be teased right now. But you can tease *me*. Just don't call me . . . noodle nose!" As a parent, you'll have to put your noodle nose to the grindstone to think up ever-sillier names.

When a child calls another child hurtful names, a parent's playfulness may turn to anger and even shame. One little girl kept telling a friend he was "stupid." When asked what she meant, the assailant said, "He isn't very bright!" Don't focus your energies on the word "stupid." Focus on what's happening *beneath* the word. Ask your child, "What's going on between you and Sam that you wanted to call him a name?" or "Did you and Sam have a disagreement today?" Look at the incident as an opportunity to find out what *really* happened and to help your child learn to regulate herself. Such children are hankering for autonomy, even as they fear their newly minted strength. Help them to use their power positively. Tell your child, "You felt very big when you said that to Sam. What other choices did you have? Next time can you find other words to help you communicate?" Sticks and stones may break bones, but certain words really *do* wound. Your child needs to know that with language comes responsibility.

What about the child who's being used as a verbal punching bag, when the game isn't lighthearted and mutual? Always take the teasing seriously, and tell the child you know how painful it is to be teased. But don't encourage her to retaliate in kind. Older children, once the subjects of taunting, say the worst response is for parents to tell teachers. Then the child being teased gets labeled further: She's a tattletale. But privately, you may urge your child to enlist a teacher on her own. You'll be helping her hone a life skill: drawing on human resources other than you.

The best approach to playground problems is to let children work them out together; they learn a great deal from getting angry at each other, as long as they're not in physical danger. Use your time at home to listen to a child who's being teased or otherwise challenged, and let her know that the calmer she is, the sooner the storm will pass. Encourage your child to gravitate toward children with whom she feels safe and, most of all, make sure she feels safe with you. Refrain from tearing down other people in front of her or belittling yourself, no matter how "stupid" you feel when you make a wrong turn or forget your keys. Always try to speak positively of your child and of other people. As the poet E. E. Cummings wrote:

> *yes is a world*
> *& in this world of*
> *yes live*
> *(Skilfully curled)*
> *all worlds*

Teach your children to live in the world of yes.

carpe diem

Advertising campaigns are always urging us to seize the moment. "Just do it!" the linebacker growls as his snarling image fills our television screen. But children truly do live in the moment, and they should. They are existential creatures whose spontaneity is even older than the Latin adage *Carpe Diem,* or "Seize the day."

Parents, on the other hand, shouldn't "just do it," if what they're about to do is change their plans. If they're going to "seize the day," it should be the day *before* a revision of their child's schedule, no matter how inconsequential the adjustment may seem. Sometimes you may not know until five minutes before that *you,* not your husband, will be driving your daughter to school that day. Tell her and ask if there's anything about the trip with Daddy— the books-on-tape you listen to, the mailboxes you count— that she'd like you to replicate. Try to give her as much control over the change as you can, without giving *in* to her. Don't be swayed by a belligerent reaction.

Whenever you can, try not to rain decrees on your child without first issuing a storm warning. This means you don't turn off the TV—for good—in the middle of *Blue's Clues*, or tell her "Mommy's not going to stay with you until you fall asleep anymore," as you're putting her into the crib. Even the smallest child is a staunch supporter of the status quo. She wants you to make her day . . . more or less the same as yesterday. Surprise may be a great tactic in war, but it's your child's enemy, and springing unpleasant news on her will cause her to rebel at the very moment you could use an ally most.

Sometimes it's you who may have to adjust your plans. You might, for instance, need to relent and remove some clothes from the bag you were giving away, now that the cherished items are too small. Sure, you could invite your friend to pick up the clothes when your toddler is out, but don't think that your little one with the elephant-sized memory won't miss her tattered tutu. Not only will she mourn its loss, she'll be angry with you for not consulting her. The top-down style of management tends to be as ineffective in parenting as it in business. Try, instead, the consensus-building approach. When your child protests, respond by acknowledging her feelings: "That tutu means a lot to you. It's a hand-me-down from your cousin, Lilly, and you're not quite ready to part with it." Next, talk about *your* feelings: "It looks uncomfortably small to me, and I feel a little embarrassed when people in this family go out of the house wearing clothes that are torn or have holes." After each of you has vented your feelings, you're ready to devise a solution to which you can both agree.

Try to treat the meeting as you would any brainstorming session with a colleague. You might even grab a pad of paper and take some notes. It helps to write suggestions down, but be sure to write them *all* down. Don't dismiss any as foolish or impractical—yet. Then review all the ideas and decide which might work best for both of you: "You said you want to keep the tutu so Lilly can see you in it when she visits next month. You also mentioned that maybe you could stop wearing it out of the house. Why don't we give it away after Lilly's visit, and until then you wear it only at home?"

Hammering out a consensus is time-consuming, but remember, what you're really doing is building a foundation of trust. That means being honest with your child and never manipulating facts that she's bound to discover anyway. Don't tell her you'll be home in "a few minutes," when you know you'll really be away for several hours. Likewise, don't postpone telling her about changes you know are inevitable, thinking you'll be able to accomplish the shift better, or with fewer tears, by springing it on her suddenly. When your proposal discomfits her, but her safety is not at issue, let her air her feelings first and try to work out a solution that accommodates you both. Seize the moment, but don't mislead or manipulate your child. She believes everything you tell her. Respect her and her faith in you by telling it like it is.

playing for keeps

the benefits of free play

Fists flying, legs flailing, bodies in a tangled, heaving mass. A football scrimmage has turned into a rumble. Only the rivals slugging it out aren't little leaguers, they're *dads*.

Sport has been heavily contested since the time of the Greeks, yet never before have parents' egos taken center stage. The cost of equipment, the grueling practice schedule, the marquee appeal of sports on a college application; all have driven up the quotient of ambition. What suffers is sport. For the youngest children, unfettered play, without the interference of coaches or parents, is as crucial to development as fresh air. The body's systems and subsystems are invigorated by muscular interaction. Left to their own devices, children spontaneously engage most of their musculoskeletal groups. But children are rarely left to their own devices anymore. They are enrolled in gymnastics classes before they can pull up their own socks. Soon even very small children are being shuffled from one formerly exotic activity to another (tae kwan do, anyone?) without regard to their level of interest or energy.

Once children could climb on their bikes and ride from yard to yard, beckoning to playmates or simply surveying their domain. Today, expectations for safety have increased even as the world has grown more dangerous: Kids are shut up in the house rather than allowed to roam, unsupervised, on the street. As a result, many children lead isolated lives, locked in their bedrooms, hunched over their Gameboy for hours on end. Their parents give them everything . . . everything but the chance to move freely. These children are motion starved.

The result, later in life, is a population plagued by chronic pain, even proud that their bodies are "hurting." That's what it means to be "tough." In fact, we are anything but tough, sheltered as we are within an invisible box. This little box defines our lives. Think of the limited range of motion required by most activities: cooking, washing dishes, making phone calls, steering the car. Our work and home environments have been adapted to the box, as has our leisure time. What do we do for fun? We rent a movie. We crawl the web. Our children, too, subsist within these parameters, given how much time they spend glued to the computer or television screen. Their imprisonment may even have psychological and neurological consequences: Some doctors argue that many children suffering from attention deficit disorder need, not drugs or counseling, but free play.

Parents who *do* take their kids to the park often see it as a substitute for step aerobics. They give themselves a workout, whipping their child from one play structure to the next. Taking your child to the park means letting her decide what *she* wants to do there, even if it's just sitting in the sandbox looking up. Let her figure out how, or if, she wants to move from the swings to the slide or whether to attempt the monkey bars. Parents often hold their little ones up to reach the bars, instead of saying, "When you're bigger, you'll be able to reach those on your own." They want their children to do justice to all the equipment, rather than to what their bodies are capable of. Parents should resist the temptation to plop a child down at the top of the slide. Invite her to make that journey on her own. You may be eager for her to experience the thrill of hurtling down, but for her the real "rush" may lie in climbing *up* the stairs. Free play means just that, "free" of expectations or goals.

Children allowed to explore the playground, or bike up and down the block, gain other advantages: They might as well be taking a crash course at the UN. They learn to negotiate with other kids, to share, to make joint decisions, even to mend disputes. Running, jumping, climbing, and digging are social skills. Within that whirling dervish— whom you recognize only by the color of her T-shirt—is a sensibility shaping and being shaped. Best of all, when kids play freely, they rarely need a parent to adjudicate. They don't need parents to become involved at all.

But playgrounds have a lot of parent-friendly equipment: secure, colorful . . . and profoundly unchallenging. The proliferation of lawsuits in recent years has led to a dumbing down of American playgrounds, and to the elimination of equipment that has multiple uses and so encourages decision making or fantasy play. Moving parts have been banished, as have overhead ladders and poles for sliding down. So, too, have tunnels that invite kids to remain hidden (briefly) from view. The ideal playground for very young children would have holes to hide in, tools to build with, wagons for hauling, and water to dam. (In Scandinavia after World War II, children were even allowed to experiment with fire, under the supervision of an adult.) It would be a place that acknowledged that play was paramount, so essential it was worth getting dirty for.

That's why parents who want to childproof the universe need to leave their drawer stops and outlet plugs at home. Parks are meant to encourage the unpredictable.

Every playground is a testing ground. "Better a broken bone than a broken spirit," said Lady Hurtwood, an early proponent of public playgrounds. She might have been counseling parents to check their fears at the entrance gate. Children need the feeling of being in control . . . and out of control, of the high-flying swing and the swooping slide. A child who experiences heightened sensations will eventually develop her own inner apparatus, so she can identify for herself when she's afraid.

Besides, most playground stunts aren't as dangerous as they seem, and many childhood accidents occur during routine play. Caution and moderation have their place in the survival of the species, but prudence should temper a child's independence, not tamp it down. Remember that play is how young children learn to negotiate their world and find a home in it. It's not about teams and rules and uniforms. In fact, the simpler or more improvised the play, the better they'll be able to amuse themselves when conditions aren't optimal (which is most of the time). So don't worry about investing in equipment or organizing carpools. There will be plenty of time for that later in life. And try never to interrupt a spontaneous game for an activity that's routinized or overdetermined. Let your kids keep on playing. They are playing for keeps.

sound and fury

spanking

Here's a dirty little secret about being a parent: We adore and cherish our little ones . . . until they piss us off by breaking our favorite mug or hitting the neighbor's child with a stick. Your three year old may be your heart's delight, but he can also upset you more quickly and completely than anyone you've ever known (other than your mate). You can try and try to squelch the anger, but sometimes that only makes it worse. "Beware the fury of a patient man," cautioned the poet John Dryden. Why? Because that fury often results in a thwack on the butt.

The idea of using the "rod" on a baby may strike many of us as extreme, but one-third of all parents begin swatting their babies on the hand or backside before their children are old enough to walk. Over 60 percent of parents condone spanking as a regular form of punishment, yet many readily concede that hitting doesn't work. If spanking does no good, why do parents persist in it? They do it out of desperation, fear ("He ran into the street and almost got killed!") or to relieve *themselves* of rage. Mainly, they do it because *their* parents did. ("My dad used to whup me, and I turned out okay.") Spanking may be the weapon you remember best from your parents' arsenal, but recall how ashamed you felt as a child when you were whacked. Striking your child—when you're angry, scared, or don't know how else to handle the situation—is an open admission that, rather than being the one in charge, *you're* out of control. When you "lose it," your child's trust in you falters. In fact, fury incarnate—your flesh meeting your child's hide—seems to have only resoundingly negative effects. Studies have shown that the more often older children (ages six to nine) are spanked, the more likely they are to lie, cheat, break things deliberately, and feel no remorse.

What many parents have in common is the desire to spare their children from being spoiled. Giving your child "something to cry about," however, won't keep him from becoming a brat. The best way to protect your child from his worst self is not to give in to his every request and not to bribe him with treats and toys to get him to behave. All toddlers have in common a need for repeated instruction. It may take days, weeks, even months for your child to stop reaching for the stove or poking his baby sister in the eye. But spanking doesn't make the lesson sink in any faster. In fact, the fear your violence inspires can stop a child from learning anything at all.

You may think that spanking a child is different from the hitting you admonish your toddler for, because it's "purposeful" and because you waited until you got home to mete out the punishment. Such justification will do little, however, to convince your confused child. After all, it's not as though he swats his buddy Chris for *no* reason, even if *his* reason might not be acceptable to you. Next time Chris grabs his bulldozer from him, he'll delay punishment just as you did: He'll wait and sock Chris when you're looking the other way. Parents who use their hands on their children but tell *them* to "use their words" would do well to heed the advice of Ralph Waldo Emerson: "What you do speaks so loudly that I cannot hear what you say."

If your child appears contrite or loving after being spanked, it's not because he understands why you struck him, but because he's relieved that your terrifying ire has subsided. You, meanwhile, may feel regret and wish that you could have resolved the matter differently. You can. If your child is about to do something dangerous or is acting "wild," use your size and strength to catch hold of him. Keep on holding him; you'll prevent him from further harm and give both of you a chance to settle down. Use the connection between your two bodies to *reconnect* and wait a few seconds before saying anything. Watch how your child surrenders to you, eventually melting in your embrace. His compliance proves once and for all that non-violence is, as Gandhi insisted, "a force more powerful."

But how can we parents model non-aggression when we feel like strangling someone? Remember that demonstrating the appropriate expression of feelings is just as important as behaving appropriately. Don't pretend to be patient when you're furious. Likewise, avoid honey-coating your rage with terms of endearment, like "sweetheart" or "precious." Give yourself permission to be angry with your child and tell him exactly how you feel. Try to keep the emphasis on *you*, which in this case means beginning with the word "I." Tell him, "*I* am *so* upset. That was a very important phone call. *I* hate being interrupted. *I* kept hearing whining even after *I* held up my hand to signal 'Quiet!' " Naked emotion, stripped of the accusatory (and mostly unnecessary) "you," is also a force more powerful. Combined with a prescription for the future, it is your best defense against similar disruptions next time.

If you're so incensed that you feel like you're going to say something hurtful ("You little brat! I just lost a client because of you"), excuse yourself from the room. Advise your child, "I need to be alone for a moment to calm down. We'll talk when I come back." If you screamed at your child—or in front of your child at the waiter who brought the wrong order for the *third* time—always tell your child you regret your behavior. Apologize to him just as you would to the waiter. The way you treat your child will be the basis of his emotional calculus for years to come.

While we may never unravel the equation of personality—the proportion of nature to nurture that defines each of us—we know that much of childhood behavior is learned. Even the gestures that seem innate, like the way your son waves his hands when he speaks or tilts his head, are habits he's picked up from you. Make sure that what your child is absorbing isn't your ragged, frustrated, or furious self, but your *best* self. And when it's not, let him know that *you* know, and that you'll try harder next time. Treat him as you would wish to be treated . . . and as you wish you *had* been treated when you were young. When you become a parent, you are offered a chance to reinvent yourself. *You* may not have been spared the rod, but you can spare your child. Your thoughtful expression of emotion, or remorse for inappropriate behavior, represents *everything* to your child: all the humane, considerate feeling that you aspire to for him and for yourself.

keeping the
peace

s i b l i n g s

Let's say your oldest son brings you some millet. Your youngest comes along next, offering you a rack of lamb. You dig into the meat, but push aside the grain harvested by your firstborn. Would it surprise you if he bore a grudge?

In the story of Cain and Abel, God took no pains to hide His preference. We parents, on the other hand, try very hard to be "fair." We describe our children as having separate but equal abilities: "Brian's good at reading, and Cory's a natural athlete." We even ignore the child dearer to our heart to "make it up" to the less fortunate one. Your affection, however, is not a zero-sum game, just as no child has a monopoly on being sloppy or polite. You don't want one child to feel he *has* to tend sheep just because the other tills soil. Think of all the seeds your shepherd won't sow if he can be only whatever his brother is not.

No child wants to be assigned a fixed role in his family's drama, just as no sibling wants to compete with the person he's also forced to share a bathroom with. While few of us would say, "Why can't you be more like your sister Caroline?" we sometimes err by pointing out how well Caroline straightened up her room or ate her greens. Holding up one child as an exemplar does injustice to both siblings, pitting them against each other and creating resentment in both. Always remember the story of Cain and Abel. You want to be sure your children are safe together if ever left alone in a field.

To keep your children from coming to blows, always acknowledge their anger. Simply listening to them is the fastest way to defuse their rage. If necessary, provide a punching bag more suitable than the other sibling. You may need to do this even when things *seem* to be going well between your toddler and his new brother. If you notice a hug turning into a wrestling hold, grab a big doll or stuffed animal and explain that he can squeeze, poke, or even hit the toy, but *not* the baby. Keep in mind that the power of his emotions and relative strength can be frightening to him. Reassure him by setting clear limits ("I won't allow your brother to get hurt") and let him know that *you* know what he's going through. "It's hard to see me paying so much attention to the baby. I can understand how you might feel jealous." Remind him that when it's time for *his* bath or bedtime, you will devote yourself to him with the same focus and care. And be sure to put aside time that's just for the two of you every day, taking him to the playground, out to dinner, or simply curling up next to him with his favorite book.

This is the biggest challenge to an older child's sense of self: the arrival of a sibling. Some have compared it to a husband who tells his mate he loves her *so* much, he wants a second wife. Don't try to simplify your firstborn's understandably complex feelings by insisting that having a baby brother is so much fun, or that you two are going to be best friends. You may be eager for your toddler to love the new baby as much as you do. And someday he will, but many days he won't.

At the moment, what he probably feels is displaced, even disconsolate. Visitors, bearing blankets and booties, will come to see the new baby, but reassure your older child that *you* see him and want him close. If he lingers nearby to watch you change or feed the baby, let him know how he can be of assistance. Say, "The baby needs a new diaper. They're in that drawer if you want to get me one," or, "I'm going to nurse him now. I wish I had my pillow. Do you know where it is?" The more you allow an older child to help, the more important he'll feel. And even though he's older and more competent, never forget that he's still a child. He may be your "big boy," but he's a tiny, striving creature, eager for your attention and uncertain of his place in the world.

But your older child can still beat the *millet* out of his younger sibling, and that may compel you to rush to the aid of your "little one" whenever the two lock horns. When parents adjudicate disputes—taking one child's side against the other—they only create more tension. The child who feels wronged doesn't blame his parents, he blames his sibling for "tattling."

How do you avoid having one child snatch toys from the other? You can't. You can only anticipate problems and talk about them before they occur . . . and again afterward, when tempers have cooled. Establish ground rules, like having each child designate "special toys" (which must be kept in a special place) and "sharing toys." Model for your older child the correct way to deal with a toddler who grabs things. Eventually he may learn to say, "I want to finish this puzzle by myself and I'm going to need all the pieces. I'm going to work up on this table where you can't reach, but here are two toys you *can* play with. Would you like to choose one?"

When an older child seems to be infringing on the rights of a younger, pre-verbal one, your only option is to work with the child who *can* articulate his point of view. If the fighting gets physical, separate the two and comfort *both* children. When you hug or stroke only the child who was hit, you reinforce their respective roles as victim and aggressor. Meanwhile, ask each sibling to tell you (or show you, in the case of a very young child) his version of what happened. Listen to what they both have to say, and repeat their words aloud, taking care to register the feelings underneath. Let your presence provide the neutral ground necessary for "meaningful exchange," but don't try to fix things. Leave the room once their grievances have been aired.

Can parents really leave two feuding siblings to work it out for themselves? It may seem heretical (even homicidal), but it's the only thing that works. Try telling your kids, "This is a tough one. I've seen you solve equally difficult problems in the past, and I'm convinced you'll come up with a way to work things out. I've got to go back and finish what I was doing. Call me if you need me again." Eventually, after months (or years) of watching you intervene impartially, your children will internalize many of your techniques and feel equipped to handle disagreements on their own.

Disagreements between siblings are inevitable, and sometimes lifelong. Why? Because siblings are often maddeningly alike. Sometimes it's what they have in common—you, for instance—that drives them apart. Your real or imagined preferences come into play even when you're not around. By removing yourself as soon as the peace process is underway, you not only expedite it, but you allow your children to take full responsibility for their success. Later in life, when they compare notes about the things you did—or didn't do—you'll be glad you helped them craft a language all their own.

But there will be times when, with or without you, your kids seem miserable together. Unfortunately, you can't be "one big, happy family" by decree. If you spend time alone with each child, you'll provide a much-needed breather from and for the others. You'll also learn to cherish what is unique in him. What you're doing is treating each child, not equally, but *separately*, showing that you know each of them has specific talents and needs. That should help with the number of explosions in your household, but there *will* be friction. For children, siblings are not only a comfort zone but a testing ground. Remind yourself that you can't reach inside your children and make them love each other or respect each other or stop stealing each other's shoes or scribbling in each other's books. You're not omnipresent, divine, nor can you ever be completely just. You're just a parent—potent though you may seem.

Rather than take your children's strife personally, equip them with the skills they need to fight fairly and reassure them that each matters enormously to you. You may never rely on one of your children to be his brother's keeper, but let them know you're counting on them to keep the peace.

the real stuff

Ever since Toto pulled back the curtain to reveal the Wizard of Oz, our reaction to technology has alternated between fascination and mistrust. In the end, the all-powerful wizard was a wimpy but well-intentioned man, looking less like a glorious potentate than . . . Bill Gates. But his heart was in the right place, as are the intentions of all the parents and teachers who worship at the altar of technology. They don't want their children, their students, to lose out or get left behind, as the indefatigable information superhighway streams past.

We are the first generation of parents for whose children technology will be transparent. We will be akin to immigrants. For us, using a computer will always require a process of translation, however instantaneous. For our children, it will be as if they've been speaking both languages—their own and cyberspeak—since birth. Given the prevalence, even dominance, of technology in our age, it may be that we don't need to expose our children to it from the time they start school. They needn't spend unlimited hours in front of the screen, playing games or doing math or alphabet drills, bathed in the computer's spooky, preternatural light.

It turns out that many of these preschoolers—yes, there are computers in the preschools—have been computer savvy even before they could speak. They have spent countless hours on the lap of a parent, enjoying a CD-ROM or just watching their parents use Quicken to pay the bills. Their interest is piqued, of course, by the fact that we seem absorbed by, even tethered to, our computers. But we recognize that technology is just a tool. Our children, however, threaten to be swallowed whole by a flood of electronic entertainment: the computers, video games, televisions, DVDs, and music systems to which they have near-unlimited access. The effect of these media is to isolate children from grown-ups, a phenomenon exacerbated by social trends like bigger houses, longer commutes, and more families in which both parents work.

Only 6 percent of sixth graders had television sets in their bedrooms in 1970; thirty years later, the number had risen to 77 percent. The average American child watches almost thirty hours of television a week. The only thing she devotes more time to is sleep. Television and video games create a simulated world where many conscientious parents fear to tread, because the violence and misogyny of what transpires there is terrifying to view. Instead, parents close their doors, and their minds, to what their kids are listening to or watching. They console themselves with the thought that at least their children are off the streets. Meanwhile, in the safety of their rooms, these kids are blowing up people and dominating small countries on the screen. The result is a generation of children suffering from a host of ills, ranging from eyestrain to severe psychological stress. (In fact, among regular computer users, visual impairment is now the norm.) At the least, a child's ride aboard the technology juggernaut is time not spent climbing the monkey bars. At worst, high-carnage video games and violent movies have been blamed for an alarming increase in rates of obesity, depression, and dependence on psychotropic drugs.

The education of our young has been a source of consternation since Plato, and the shadows on the cave wall in *The Republic* might as well have been images lurking on a computer or television screen. Parents of older children should rouse them from *their* cave—or bedroom—and compel them to engage in group activities out-of-doors. Televisions and computers should be placed only in communal areas, where parents can monitor their use. Parents can also exercise control by setting limits on where their children can surf on the web or by automatically shutting down an account at a certain hour every night. Best of all, parents should talk with their children about games or videos that promote violence or racism, just as they can teach their children to think critically about the advertising they absorb on television.

But for very young children, the use of media is even more complicated because their filters are less well developed. They don't always know what's "real." Studies have shown that many children under five don't realize television advertising isn't part of their program. Kids need you to sit beside them, talking a blue streak, asking them questions, and interpreting for them. (Yes, you would throw popcorn at such a person if he sat next to you at the movies. But your child's mental health is worth becoming a pest.) Very small children learn by *doing*, not by tuning in or logging on. They need to manipulate, to participate, to transform things, not to be transfixed by them.

Some educators believe preschoolers learn only through interactions that involve the whole body. Others think that very young children can go well beyond sensation and action to understand the world in an abstract way. They applaud the use of technology in the classroom but not at the expense of reading specialists or art and physical education activities. They consider computers just one of a host of learning tools; in truth, there is little evidence that computers "teach" better than conventional methods.

Some studies even suggest that digital instruction *hinders* brain development by reducing opportunities for thinking aloud, asking questions, and solving problems creatively. At the least, educators should resist pressure from computer manufacturers and software companies to promote computers as indispensable learning tools. (Almost $4 billion a year is spent putting computers in classrooms, even as music classes and math books are excised from the school budget.) It turns out that the most efficient, cost-effective, user-friendly materials are still found bound between book covers. They don't hum or bleat or beckon, except passively. Does anyone remember books?

Every time you reach for a newspaper, or look up a word in the dictionary, you remind your child that there are other paths to information. You demonstrate that learning is not just about processing data. As one writer put it, the book falls open, and the reader falls in. Books create worlds, from Tibet to Togo, that a child can hold in her hands. She sees faces, she hears foreign words, she learns of distant customs and cultures. And she can recapture the experience, exactly and never the same, every time she opens the book. But very young children need us to be there with them, to snuggle close to them, to bring these worlds alive. Long before we teach them to read, we are teaching them to *want* to read by demonstrating how captivating books can be.

You should offer your child a rich menu of reading material, just as you vary her daily diet: some poetry, some nonfiction, even the daily comics or a book of recipes. In doing so, you are accommodating her ear to language that she won't hear on the playground: *literary* language. It swoops and darts and swirls and dances and spins. When actors learn to recite Shakespeare, they become accustomed, sometimes with difficulty, to the daunting march of the iambic pentameter. But soon, when they perform, if they go "up" and forget their lines, they may fill in with a word or phrase that exactly captures the rhythm and intonation. The difficult poetry becomes second nature, the *only* way to say what they need to say. Similarly, young children to whom parents or teachers read poetry sometimes slip into "literary language." They will startle you by using words like "dwell" or "actually" or comment on their mother's "rosy lips" with as much sincerity as any hero in *The Iliad*.

What you want, more than a child who can recite Longfellow, is a child who possesses an almost infinite variety of tools. She can reach beyond herself to express an emotion or to share an insight. She knows, not just her own culture and customs, but about the poetry of the Inuit or what an okapi eats. Parents often shy away from the "classics," *Charlotte's Web* or *A Little Princess*, because they worry about grotesque imagery or the subject of death. You'll know if your child can cope with those themes as you progress. Don't censure stories to protect *yourself* from something too challenging. But don't insist on reading your child all the "great" books because you loved them. She may be interested in bats or trains, not princesses. Stop often to inquire about what's happening in the book, to make sure your child understands. Don't hesitate to go "back" to simpler books, especially if they are among your child's favorites. The predictability of a much-loved story is one of its pleasures. You'll know if the reader snuggled next to you is bored.

More often, you will notice that your child is a more than careful listener. She'll correct you when you change an "a" to "the." She begins to own the book, to predict what will happen, to want to turn the page. Encourage her. Stop and examine the illustrations. Ask, "What do you think is happening in that picture?" And don't be afraid to skip long, descriptive passages if you think your little one is not up to them yet. Trust her imagination to catch, and cherish, the most important points. Always recite the book's title, and its author and illustrator, no matter how many times you've read the book. That will help set the stage for what's to unfold.

Your children, as ever, will take their cues from you. Do you pick up a newspaper at night or turn on the television? Do you have a laptop on your bedside table or a stack of books? Never forget that what most intrigues a child about any activity is your involvement. Whatever it is, you should participate. Don't let her play on the computer for long periods unsupervised. If you need to turn on your laptop, place an old manual typewriter or an extra computer keyboard in the same room; your child can bang away on it with the same pleasure and purpose you bring to your work. Or encourage your child to open a book, to "read" to herself, or to make up stories or plays inspired by what you've read. Next time you see a spider, you might wonder aloud if she's a great-granddaughter of Charlotte's. When you eat a piece of chocolate, ask your child if Mr. Wonka helped to manufacture it. Reading to your children will create worlds of correspondence between you, inspiring art projects and cascades of private jokes. As the poet W. S. Merwin wrote:

> *What we are looking for*
> *In each other*
> *Is each other*

What your child wants most in the world from you . . . is you. Nothing simulated can recreate the warmth of your presence, the excitement of your involvement. You, and you alone, are the real stuff.

footprints

the search for identity

We are who we are from the moment we're born, but the process of *discovering* who we are can last a lifetime. No sooner do we leave the womb than the world begins to classify us, assigning us Apgar scores to rate our vital signs. Our lives are filled with numbers, many of which define us, from social security numbers to SAT scores and credit ratings. But nothing better identifies us than the tiny, tender footprint that once adorned our birth certificates.

In fact, our recorded history is inscribed with footprints. Some last only as long as the next wave; others are around for a good. . . . 3.6 million years. If you go to Laetoli, Tanzania, you will see fossilized footprints from one of our earliest ancestors. This upright predecessor, yet to invent a tool, stopped in her tracks and looked back. Was she checking for danger, measuring the distance traveled, or studying her own impression upon the earth like a child walking on wet sand?

Some day, while strolling by the sea, your child will stop to examine *his* footprint. He'll want to see how it's different from yours, as well as from the stranger's who walked along the same beach an hour earlier. Your child will be looking for clues to the age-old question, "Who am I?" and his search, which becomes more pronounced and urgent in adolescence, can be troubling. Our children's quest fills us with anxiety because we have painful memories of—or are still engaged in—our own struggle. Besides, who knows our children better than we do? We like to tell them who they are ("You make friends easily" or "You're good at sports"), the same way we tell them how to open a carton of milk, rather than letting them figure it out on their own. Just because your child did something "well" last month doesn't mean he will again, or even wants to. The skill you've singled out may be of little significance to him.

We offer children our opinion of them, but opinions are like fossils, petrified observations. To be a child is to be in flux. Always telling your child, "You're a great artist" is like telling your partner, "You never take out the trash." Beware of statements that categorize or reduce because the person you're categorizing may well stop listening. And listening is something children love to do, especially if the story you're embarking on is about them.

"Tell me again about when I was a baby," urges even the youngest child, as if it were ancient history. Listening, he marvels at the miles he's traveled and delights in our pleasure at recounting his past. But these "highlights" are *your* highlights, what you are able to remember or choose to recount. If your child ever writes his autobiography, you might find that the stories you enjoy telling don't even appear, or that the "facts" are altered. Likewise, the photographs your child grows up viewing on the mantle are the memories you've selected for display, not the moments he might otherwise recall.

Mother Nature, too, takes snapshots—the footprints at Laetoli are some—but they don't necessarily mark momentous occasions. Even though fossils take millennia to form, they are spontaneous, random, like the moments that may matter most to your child. That's why you don't want to edit his emotions—even when they lead to struggle or self-doubt. When your child's searching for answers, refrain from rushing in to fill the "void." Many of us prefer to ignore our children's negative feelings or cover them up by "looking at the bright side." Difficult as it may seem, your job is also to shed light on his darkness. Your observations, rather than your judgments, will be most illuminating.

There will be times in your child's life when he won't know if he's coming or going. Still, he must make his own tracks. Remember that a footprint, whether fresh or fossilized, is like a crescent moon, defined as much by what's missing as by what is visible. Someday, using all that he is and all that he isn't, your child will make his own indelible mark on the world.